Charlie 2-1 Bravo

Charlie 2-1 Bravo

*Memoir of a Drunken
Paratrooper in Afghanistan*

E.E. Summerfield

McFarland & Company, Inc., Publishers
Jefferson, North Carolina

LIBRARY OF CONGRESS CATALOGUING-IN-PUBLICATION DATA

Names: Summerfield, E. E., 1984– author.
Title: Charlie 2–1 Bravo : memoir of a drunken paratrooper in Afghanistan / E.E. Summerfield.
Description: Jefferson, North Carolina : McFarland & Company, Inc., Publishers, 2020 | Includes index.
Identifiers: LCCN 2020023844 | ISBN 9781476682174 (paperback) ∞
    ISBN 9781476640310 (ebook)
Subjects: LCSH: Summerfield, E. E., 1984– | United States. Army. Parachute Infantry Regiment, 508th. Company C. | Afghan War, 2001—Campaigns—Afghanistan—KandahaÄÑr (Province) | Afghan War, 2001—Personal narratives, American. | United States. Army—Military life—History—Afghan War, 2001– | Soldiers—United States—Biography.
Classification: LCC DS371.413 .S86 2020 | DDC 958.104/74092 [B]—dc23
LC record available at https://lccn.loc.gov/2020023844

BRITISH LIBRARY CATALOGUING DATA ARE AVAILABLE

ISBN (print) 978-1-4766-8217-4
ISBN (ebook) 978-1-4766-4031-0

© 2020 E.E. Summerfield. All rights reserved

No part of this book may be reproduced or transmitted in any form or by any means, electronic or mechanical, including photocopying or recording, or by any information storage and retrieval system, without permission in writing from the publisher.

Front cover: The author sitting in a fighting position for the last time in his military career (Brandon Young); *background* Afghanistan mountains © 2020 Shutterstock

Printed in the United States of America

McFarland & Company, Inc., Publishers
  Box 611, Jefferson, North Carolina 28640
   www.mcfarlandpub.com

Table of Contents

Preface   1
Terms   5
Battalion Structure   7

1. Black Outs and Black Ops   9
2. With No Training and Little Intel   19
3. Snap-Backs and Taliban?   28
4. Farming for Taliban   42
5. IEDs for Sale or Trade   51
6. Kotizi   56
7. Unexpected Company   70
8. Jelly Legs   75
9. Seek and Defecate   82
10. Gundi Ghar   87
11. Gundi Ghar, Day Two   96
12. Chapman   115
13. The Return to Gundi Ghar   119
14. Back to the Grind   129
15. Deegan Cole   133
16. The Complexities of My Emotions   139
17. To Check or Not to Check   148
18. Ice Cream and Lattes   155

19. But Nobody Died, Right?	158
20. Night on the Big Town	162
21. Superheroes with Drinking Problems	169
22. Now Let's Never Do That Again	181
23. Bargaining for Your Future	185
Index	193

Preface

This story came to be in order to provide the reader with a look into the life of the lower-ranked enlisted soldiers in today's United States Army. There are many military memoirs told from the point of view of high-ranking officers and members of the special operations community. While they are great works, they fail to capture what it's like for the majority of those in the combat arms professions. Thus, this work is written about the day-in and day-out grind that is the plight of the privates and specialists, those doing the dirty work both literally and figuratively. These individuals have no real say over what they do, say, wear, or even think in an average day.

In order to best tell this story, I purposefully left out the names of all the leadership in my chain of command. As discussed above, this work is about the lower enlisted. It was my goal to exclude every leader I possibly could. This is not because I do not respect them, or don't think that they contributed to the cause. Quite the contrary; in fact, I can say with great certainty that their actions kept every soldier in my platoon alive. That said, I chose to keep them nameless because this is not their story. I wanted to tell a story about the guys who no one listens to. I wanted to tell this story from the perspective of the guy who has to do 500 pushups because someone in his platoon wore white socks instead of green socks.

This perspective is unique because these individuals have very little if anything to lose. Officers are concerned about promotions, and senior NCOs are trying not to get demoted before they retire. A bunch of privates who get in trouble five times a day no matter what they do have a propensity to risk it all. Whether they risk it all on the battlefield or in a nightclub makes no difference to them. As a matter of fact, I have been in far more dangerous situations day-drinking with paratroopers Stateside than on patrol in Afghanistan.

I feel that it is important to note that this work is a compilation of a journal that I kept throughout my time in the Army. It is thanks to this journal that I am able to recount these stories with such clarity. Had I not had the forethought to jot down my experiences shortly after they occurred, this work probably never would have come to be. I had a great deal of help with this memoir as well. Many a soldier from my time in the Army helped check my work by telling me his side of the story. Thus, with the help of my journal and my friends, I have completed this memoir as accurately as I possibly could. A benefit of having written many of these stories immediately following their occurrence is the tone that the chapters take on. It seems to me that the reader can sense the mood I was in when I wrote the chapter. When I was angry or hopeful, that comes through in the reading.

Additionally, I worked very hard to protect everyone's privacy throughout this process. I used pseudonyms for all but a select few who have asked to remain identifiable. I didn't include any photos of anyone whose permission I did not obtain. So, if you didn't ask to be named and you find yourself reading this work and think that you didn't say or do that, you are correct. I didn't use your likeness or name, so you didn't say or do that.

I worked to keep this book as short as possible and broke it down into two parts. Those two parts consist of operations that required a bulletproof vest and those that required 100 proof. These two types of operations completely encompass how I spent my time in the Army. If I wasn't training or on deployment, I was out on the town with the other lower enlisted hooligans in my unit.

Another important note to add is that I was not able to include all of the paratroopers that I wanted in the book. At first, I tried to include everyone in the platoon, but the story become unbelievably cumbersome. Trying to follow thirty-plus individuals in and out of patrols and missions was just short of impossible. In the end, I felt it best to include the few people that I knew the best during this time in my life. I feel that this allows the story to be as true as I could make it to what I experienced. Ultimately it is my story, told from my perspective as I lived it. It could have been told from three dozen different perspectives, but it just happens to be told from the tiny insignificant security sector from which I viewed it.

Lastly, I want to make it very clear how I feel about all the people I served with during this deployment. Even if I hated you while I was in the Army, I still respect you as a soldier and as an American. Even though it pains me to admit it, I knew everyone I went on patrol with would be there for me if I needed help. Even if you were one of the soldiers that I didn't get along with, I knew you would be there. I learned a great deal from everyone that I knew in the military, and I would not trade my experiences for anything.

"It doesn't take a hero to order men into battle. It takes a hero to be one of those men who goes into battle."
—General Norman Schwarzkopf, Jr.

Terms

ACH	Army Combat Helmet
AG	Assistant Gunner
ALP	Afghan Local Police
ANA	Afghan National Army
AO	Area of Operations
BIP	Blast in Place
CAB	Combat Action Badge
CIB	Combat Infantry Badge
CMB	Combat Medic Badge
COIST	Company Intelligent Support Team
COP	Combat Outpost
DM	Designated Marksman
DUI	Driving Under the Influence
ECP	Entry Control Point
EOD	Explosive Ordnance Disposal
FO	Forward Observer
FOB	Forward Operating Base
HEDP	High Explosive Dual Purpose
HLZ	Helicopter Landing Zone
HUMVEE	High Mobility Multipurpose Wheeled Vehicle
IED	Improvised Explosive Device
KA-BAR	Combat Knife
KAF	Kandahar Air Field
KIA	Killed in Action
LMTV	Light Medium Tactical Vehicle
MATV	Military All-Terrain Vehicle
MaxxPro MRAP	Mine Resistance Armor Protected

MRE	Meal Ready to Eat
NCO	Noncommissioned Officer
NTC	Northern Training Center
OP	Outpost
PKM	Pulemyot Kalashnikova Modernizirovany (General Purpose Machine Gun)
PL	Platoon Leader
POGs	People Other than Grunts
PSG	Platoon Sergeant
PT	Physical Training
RPG	Rocket-Propelled Grenade
RTO	Radio Telephone Operator
SAW	Squad Automatic Weapon
SOG	Sergeant of the Guard
TC	Truck Commander
THOR	Man-portable, Counter-radio-controlled (IED) Jammer
U.S.	United States

Battalion Structure

I designed the following diagram to briefly explain the structure of a battalion, for readers who may not be familiar with military organization. Each company and platoon is constructed similarly, even though I have only included one example of each. I understand it can be difficult to follow along with some of the unit designations. However, I did not want to weigh the book down with long explanations within the narrative.

If at any point in time you find yourself wondering why a company just showed up or why a faceless being is giving me orders, that is much the way I felt during this deployment. Information is often passed down six or more times before it reaches the privates and the specialists in a platoon. I could not have picked my battalion commander out of a line of other commanders. I rarely interacted with anyone above my rank, and when I did, that person rarely exceeded the rank of staff sergeant.

Battalion Structure

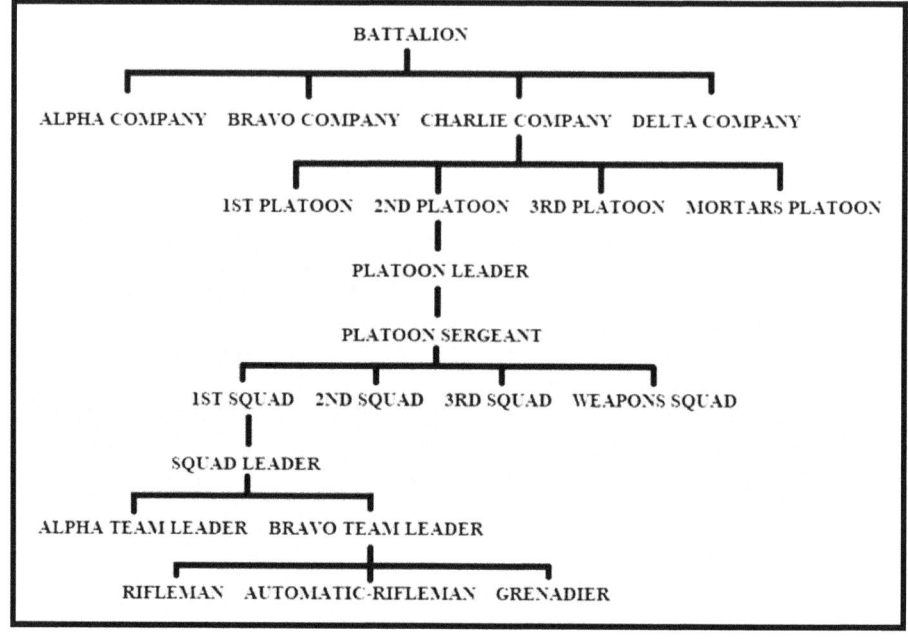

Basic structure of an infantry battalion.

– 1 –

Black Outs and Black Ops

April 11, 2015

"So, let me get this straight. Your brother leaves for Basic Training tomorrow, you get out of the Army tonight at midnight, and ... it's my fucking birthday?" Lemmon asked, pointing his finger at me and then Nate, with a weird smile on his face.

"That pretty much sums it up," Nate said with a bit of a confused shrug.

"And?" I asked, egging Lemmon on with a hand gesture.

"Are we going to just sit in this apartment all night or are we going to celebrate, you bunch of slack-jawed Nancies?" Lemmon yelled, throwing his hands into the air dramatically.

"Well, we can go have a drink, but I don't need to get wasted. We have to be up at 0600 in the morning to take him to the recruiting office," I said with just a hint of hesitation.

"No no no. Just a few drinks, that's all," Lemmon said with an obvious wink in Nate's direction.

"I don't care where we go, I just expect you guys to tell me some damn good war stories. I need to get all pumped up before I ship off to Basic," Nate said as he made his way to the door.

"Well get in the goddamn truck. We're burnin' daylight, men!" Lemmon yelled as he mocked kicking Nate in the ass out the door.

As I locked up behind us, I knew all I had to do was keep the night from getting too out of control. Just a few drinks, then I'll come home. No big deal, no more fucking Nashvilles. I'm way too old for this high-level boozing.

* * *

Big Al's Tavern was just a short ten-minute drive from my apartment. Al's tavern was known for two things: wings, and those tiny bandana-shaped halter tops that the waitresses wore. Seeing it was our usual hangout, we decided to start the night out there. As we walked into Al's, the hostess stepped up to greet us, only to be interrupted by Lemmon. He never broke stride as he passed by her, waving his hand and pointing towards something behind her. He didn't need a table because they had all he needed at the bar. Coming to understand the man's objective, she just smiled, took a step back, and waved us on through.

Lemmon pulled up a barstool, motioned for Nate to take a seat, and then ordered three shots of tequila and three PBR tallboys. You could tell by the look on Nate's face that he was unimpressed. He had heard all sorts of crazy stories about Lemmon and me power-drinking, getting into gunfights, and jumping out of airplanes. Seeing drink orders like this led him to believe they were just a bunch of fairy tales. His skepticism prompted him to smile, pound the shot, and then look Lemmon directly in the eyes. This was his way of challenging him to some kind of drinking contest.

Watching the challenge transpire, I couldn't help but stare at the two of them with stern disapproval. I really didn't want to wake up in the back of a van being taken to an undisclosed location again. All I had to do was survive the night and I'd finally be a free man. No more formations, no more PT, no more fighting positions. Just survive the night.

"Well, tough guy, those shots were for a toast, not for you to pound. And if dad's not going to cry about too much booze, we can get as fucked up as you want," Lemmon said, staring right back at Nate.

With that, they both turned towards me as if waiting for approval. To which I sighed, looked at my watch, and held up three fingers and then two. The bartender nodded and made up three double shots of Jack Daniels, since she knew what I always ordered. Nate, liking where the night was headed, then took Lemmon's shot, pounded, it and turned towards the bartender, eagerly awaiting his next drink.

"Well, slow down there, Nate, there's plenty of booze to go around," Lemmon said as the bartender set the shots down in front of us. Now Lemmon could propose a proper toast as he had intended with the first round.

"Here's to the unrelenting sadness that awaits the younger Summerfield," Lemmon said raising his glass.

* * *

As I stared at the ordering screen behind the bar, everything was just a bit too blurry. I could barely make out the buttons that I needed to push

1. Black Outs and Black Ops

to order three more shots of Jack. As I finished my order, Amber the bartender yelled for me to punch two tallboys in on the screen for her. I had consumed just enough booze to make this simple task quite difficult.

"Does he do this all the time, just go back there and work behind the counter?" Nate asked Lemmon as the two of them laughed at me.

"Only when he is really drunk," Lemmon answered, taking a swig of his beer. "They don't seem to mind the help. Supposedly they ordered him one of those bandana tops, but he has never worn it," Lemmon added, laughing.

"Oh, he has, no doubt," Nate chuckled.

As they laughed at my part-time profession, I made my way back around the bar. Setting the drinks down in front of the two men, I took a stool next to them. Sipping on my drink, I decided that we needed to come up with a foolproof plan of action while the night was still young.

"You know, hamp, I thought you might decide that, and I was thinking. Nate here has never been to Vixen's," Lemmon explained, turning to face me.

"It is a fine establishment," I stated in a matter-of-fact tone.

"I thought you guys were going to tell me some war stories," Nate said, interrupting us.

We decided that the war stories could wait and that we needed to take Nate to Vixen's. Which was, of course, the most glorious strip club a poor enlisted man could afford to frequent. Having drunk way too much to drive, Lemmon began to drunk-dial our favorite cab driver. While he struggled to outsmart the keypad on his phone, I came up with a brilliant idea. We could just walk, since it was only like a mile from Al's. All we had to do was take that shortcut through the little wood line by the car dealership. I had never taken this route before (a fact that I harmlessly kept to myself), but I just knew that it would take us exactly where we wanted to go. Nate was indifferent to the idea; Lemmon, on the other hand, had some concerns. He was willing to walk if and only if my shortcut would allow us to bypass Bargain Street. He was absolutely adamant about avoiding that treacherous stretch of asphalt. It took a little convincing, but after I guaranteed that we wouldn't come anywhere near the dreaded Bargain Street, Lemmon finally agreed to take the shortcut.

I had squared us up with the house while I was behind the counter, so we finished our beers and made our way to the door. Lemmon was so giddy when he jumped up from his stool, he collided with some poor waitress. She had a full tray of forty-some-odd wings suspended over her head, and she barely kept from spilling them everywhere.

With that near miss we exited, crossed the street, and headed towards the infamous shortcut. The only thing that stood between us was a small, thickly wooded area that had a chain-link fence running through the middle. As we approached, I thought that people must cut through here all the time, since the fence looked like a natural line of drift. All we had to do was follow it in one side and out the other. As we skirted the fence further into the wood line, the briers and vines continued to get thicker and thicker. At some points they were so dense I had to stop and break brush to push forward.

As I was hacking my way through some particularly stubborn vines, I heard what sounded like running water. After a closer look, I came to realize there was a rather large ravine blocking our path to Vixen's. The chain-link fence that we were skirting ran from one side of the ravine to the other. Luckily for us, it created a makeshift bridge that we could use to cross. "No problem for a ninja like me," I thought. I would jump to the chain-link fence and use it to traverse the 30-meter gap. Then we could keep pushing on through to the other side of what had now become a miniature jungle. Once through the vines, I took two steps, jumped to the fence and started to shimmy across. As I reached the middle, Nate stopped at the edge of the ravine. He was seriously starting to doubt that I had ever taken this shortcut before. Lemmon, on the other hand, had the utmost faith in my navigation skills. So he ran past Nate, who was still standing at the ravine, and then jumped to the fence.

Once on the other side, Lemmon and I noticed that Nate had yet to start the crossing. Not wanting to miss the midnight dance specials, we yelled for him to get a move on with it. He hesitantly made the jump and started to shimmy across on what looked like a very unsteady grip.

Growing more and more impatient, Lemmon and I started to encourage Nate along by insulting his masculinity, using all the colorful terms and linguistic gems that we had acquired in our five long years in the infantry. Despite our encouragement, Nate decided it best that he stop halfway across the ravine and take a short break.

"I don't think that's actually resting," Lemmon laughed as Nate shook his hands one at a time, resting his grip.

"Just get close and grab my hand," Lemmon said as he grabbed the fence with one hand and reached out with the other.

I impatiently watched as Nate inched his way across, every few feet seeing if he could reach Lemmon's outstretched hand. After a few attempts, he got into a position that was just outside of Lemmon's grasp. Nate then stretched his arm out as far as he possibly could in an attempt at covering

1. Black Outs and Black Ops

the last few inches. You could tell that he was doing all he could so as not to have to move again. Just as I thought Nate was going to make it, his grip failed and he plummeted towards the bottom of the ravine! As Nate hurtled toward certain death, Lemmon dove flat onto his stomach and plunged his arm into the darkness below! I knew there was no way Lemmon could catch him. Having heard no impact, I stood there motionless, wondering just how far he had fallen. Somehow in total darkness Lemmon managed to catch Nate's hand and prevent him from plunging to his doom.

"Are you close to the bottom?" Lemmon asked, hoping to be able to set him down gently.

"Fuck no! I can't even see the bottom. I'm just hanging here by your arm," Nate said, surprised at how deep the ravine actually was.

Pulling his feet under him, Lemmon got into a position that allowed him to slowly drag Nate up from the depths of imminent demise. Once back on solid ground, the three of us ever so carefully approached the edge of the ravine. Peering into the darkness below provided us with no idea as to the depth of the pit. Following a brief moment of reflection, we pushed ever onward towards our objective. Vixen's!

Nate was now certain I had never taken this shortcut before. He was getting tired of this little adventure and wanted to know how much farther we had to go. I of course assured him that it was just around the corner. All we had to do was jump a massive razor-wire fence that now blocked our path. I just knew that Vixen's would be right on the other side of that fence. As he heard this, he turned toward Lemmon and shook his head in disapproval. Lemmon just shrugged and smiled.

As he was brushing the dirt off his shirt, Nate was starting to wonder whether they would even let us in this place. After all, we had been traipsing through the jungle for more than an hour by this point. He didn't know this fine establishment like Lemmon and I did. He was seriously overestimating the dress code. Lemmon once carried me into Vixen's when I was too drunk to walk in of my own power. They just asked him if he had the cover charge for his buddy and they let the both of us right on in.

Before we could pay a cover, however, we still had to cross that razor-wire fence. I was the first to it, and like the ninja I was, I shimmied up a tree next to it. I then stepped on one of the razor-wire support beams and used it to vault to the other side. As my feet made contact with the ground, I used a combat roll to break the 10-foot fall. Lemmon was up next and not nearly as graceful in his jeans and cowboy boots. He made it up the tree and over the top of the razor wire just fine. The shimmy down to my side proved to be much more difficult. Using a tree and the fence to slide down did nothing but hopelessly tangle his pant leg up in the razor wire.

After a few tugs, Lemmon realized that it was not going to break free easily. So he secured himself with both hands on a branch from the tree that he had been using to reach my side. Doing so moved him into a position that was completely horizontal to the ground. Hanging there upside down, he looked like a three-toed sloth preparing to take a nap. After a brief rest, he started to violently kick downwards in a futile attempt at freeing himself. Watching him struggle like a coyote in a bear trap, I decided that I should go help. Standing up from my kneeling position where I had stopped at the end of my combat roll, I headed to Lemmon's aid.

During my short walk to where he was hanging, Lemmon managed to get his other boot stuck in the wire. This only worked to infuriate him and prompted him to kick even more wildly. Just as I started to tell him to hold still, he kicked downward with all of his might. The force of the kick proved to be more than he needed. As his pants broke free, the fence slingshotted one of those cowboy boots directly into my solar plexus. It looked like I got hit by one of those old wind-up action figures with crotch-kicking action. The blow to the chest flung me backwards, and I crashed into a van that seemed to come out of nowhere. He had knocked the wind completely out of me! As I struggled to catch my breath, he didn't even notice that he had delivered a devastating cross kick to my sensitive little tummy. Lemmon just continued to struggle like a madman in a strait jacket. As he flailed about angrily, the branch that held his weight broke, and he plummeted the ten feet to the ground. Landing flat on his back, he got a taste of his own medicine, both of us now desperately searching for air.

As Lemmon and I laid on the ground struggling to catch our breath, Nate jumped down from the fence and landed between us.

"What the fuck are you two idiots doing?" Nate asked, clearly annoyed.

"Fighting the war on terrorism," I replied, half out of breath.

"I thought we were almost there," Nate said, taking in his surroundings.

"Yeah, this looks a lot like a secure compound to me," Lemmon said, moving into position next to me by the van.

Surveying the scene, I could see several small windowless buildings and vehicles sporadically positioned around a compound of some sort. It was, of course, surrounded by the razor-wire fence that we had just vaulted over. There were several spotlights that were focused on the corners of the razor wire as well. This was intelligently done, as these would be the areas easiest for intruders to cross. Seeing as we were the intruders, we would need to hit one of the corners if we wanted to exit the other side of the compound towards Vixen's. There was about 200 meters of terrain in between us and the nearest exit. Considering the totality of the situation, Nate was not sure our best course of action was to push onward.

"It's either that or back across that ravine, cave diver," I said, slapping Lemmon on the back and laughing hysterically at my own joke.

"Goddammit!" Nate said, resigning himself to push forward.

With the decision made, Lemmon and I took up positions behind cover and started to size up the situation. Lemmon decided all we had to do was stick to the shadows and use the small outbuildings as cover. This would allow us to get within striking distance of the crossing point unseen. While he explained his plan, he pointed out which buildings he thought would provide us with the safest route. Deciding Lemmon had come up with the most reasonable plan a drunk paratrooper could have come up with, I took point. I then combat-rolled into the first spot that offered good concealment from the spotlights. Now all the other two troops had to do was start bounding maneuvers and we would be at the strip club in no time.

Lemmon smiled, motioned for Nate to go next, and then took up rear security to ensure no one came up on our six. As we continued to make drunken bounds toward our objective, Lemmon and I were laughing and doing shitty combat rolls in and out of our positions like a bunch of B-movie Navy Seals, whereas Nate took a more serious and annoyed fatherly approach to the process.

Once we were within striking distance of the corner, we regrouped to come up with a plan. Before we could fully formulate Operation Dash to Freedom, we heard some people coming out of one of the buildings to our right. Realizing that we were not alone, the three of us lay motionless in the shadows under a small overhang. From our hiding spot we could see two men dressed in what looked like security uniforms. We could tell that they were arguing about something, but they were too far away to make out what they were saying. One of the men kept pointing in our direction and shaking his hands wildly. This was a pretty good indicator that they had heard us doing our shitty Black Op. After a short lovers' spat, they seemed to come to an agreement of some sort, and they both went toward separate buildings. Just as I was about to breathe a sigh of relief, I heard the sound of barking dogs! To make matters worse, the man who had been pointing in our direction returned with two M4s. Seeing this,

Lemmon and I started to giggle, and Nate got even more pissed off by our inability to take anything seriously.

I think Lemmon was the first to realize that we may actually be in a bit of a pickle. We either had to make a run for the corner right then or head back the way we came. Once those Rottweilers entered the field of play, there was no way we would all three be able to cross that fence corner.

"We had better head back now that they actually have rifles and dogs. We will never be able to climb that fence fast enough to keep from someone getting shot in the ass," I said, thinking back to the Cirque du Soleil performance we had executed on the fence earlier.

As Lemmon and Nate nodded in agreement, the sound of dogs barking let us all know that it was time to go.

"Holy shit, they actually have dogs and guns!" Lemmon laughed, slapping Nate on the shoulder as he took a knee next to me in preparation to move out.

The bounds back were still full of shitty combat rolls and baseball slides, but we managed to stay relatively quiet. Reaching the fence, I told Nate to jump it first, since it had taken him the longest to cross the first time. He climbed up the tree next to the fence and started his way down the other side as Lemmon watched our six. Thankfully, this part of the compound was thickly wooded, and we were shielded from view. As long as we jumped the fence before the dogs got to us, we should be fine. I felt it unlikely the men would chase us once we were out of the compound.

On his way down the tree on the opposite side of the fence, Nate got his pants hopelessly stuck in the razor wire. Despite his best efforts, he could not for the life of him get free. So I again decided someone needed my help. Once to the top of the fence, I made my way across the upright beams to where Nate was stuck. I then proceeded to stomp on Nate's boot, pants and leg in a desperate and hilarious attempt at freeing him from the evil clutches of the insidious fence. With each stomp I executed, I did everything but free Nate's leg. I bruised his calf, tore his pants and pissed him off.

While we were doing this, Lemmon just kept saying, "Gotta hurry. Gotta hurry." We could all hear the barking dogs rapidly approaching our position.

With Lemmon urging him on, Nate decided to jump down, pant leg and all still attached. As his massive 230-lb. frame crash landed in the bushes below, a great deal of his pants decided to stay with the fence. With

1. Black Outs and Black Ops

Nate down and the sound of barking dogs fast approaching, I dived over him into some tall bushes. Followed right behind me was Lemmon, who hit the ground running. He headed straight back towards the ravine we had crossed earlier. Never breaking stride, he just jumped, grabbed the fence and flew across it like a pro. I waved for Nate to follow suit as I took up rear security, the sound of barking dogs hot on our coattails.

Nate reluctantly took back across the ravine with me right behind him. Gripping the chain-link fence was a little more difficult now since I was all sweaty. This made me consider the fact that Nate could fall, but I laughed it off as another funny part of my already hilarious day. Once Nate reached the middle of the ravine, he again stopped to shake his hands out and rest.

"Go, motherfucker, there is no time to rest!" I said, nagging him on.

"Give me a second I gotta rest, man," he said, annoyed by my haste.

"You can't rest just hanging over a precipice," I said, making a lisp-like sound as if to emphasize my point.

After what seemed like an eternity of bickering, my grip strength started to waver. Nate had made me wait there for so damn long I was starting to worry that I may fall now. Just as I decided that I would have to go back and rest, Nate finally pushed onward. With my path clear of obstacles, I traversed the last 15 meters of the ravine. Come to find out there was a tiny drain pipe that was sticking out just below the chain-link fence. Nate was using it as a resting point both times he crossed the ravine. He was just standing there resting his ass off while I held myself up with the power of my grip alone.

Once on the other side, we rejoined Lemmon and took up a slight jog in a single-file line. Like the good troops we were, we ensured we had perfect 10-meter intervals in between each man and the next. As we reached the road where we had started, we return to an unorganized gaggle. At that time, Nate made it clear he was unimpressed with our shenanigans.

"All I wanted to do was drink some beer and hear some war stories! But nooo, you two assholes lead us on a wild goose chase where we have to fight off dogs and armed guards. Not to mention the fact that we are literally right back where we started!" Nate said as he took in the damage to his shirt and pants.

"Well, the good news is that we can start the war stories here, because we have a bit of a walk now that my shortcut has turned into a long cut," I said, laughing and pointing at Lemmon.

"What's so funny?" Lemmon asked.

"Looks like we are headed down Bargain Street, little buddy," I said, still laughing at Lemmon.

"God dammit, hamp!" Lemmon said, looking around as if something might sneak up behind him. Motioning for me to take the lead, he added, "Well, start this story from the beginning, troop. We've got a way to go before the bargains begin."

– 2 –

With No Training and Little Intel

I arrived at my Parachute Infantry Regiment late in October of 2011. This was a few short months before the unit's 2012 deployment to Afghanistan. I, like several others in the unit, was a Special Forces dropout. For those who don't know, one can join the Army and participate in what is known as the 18X-ray program. This allows one to try out for Special Forces, but if one should fail at any point in the training pipeline, he will be sent to a regular infantry unit or line unit, as we call it.

One funny thing about all the other dropouts was that they always had a long, sad story about why they hadn't made it through their training pipeline. They had got hurt, or the instructors were out to get them. It was never their fault. Not me, though; I had failed of my own accord, and only wished someone had told me I was going to before I had joined the Army. If I had known that I wasn't tough, smart, or physically fit before I joined, it would have saved me a whole hell of a lot of trouble.

Within the regiment, I was sent to Charlie Company, second platoon, or Two Charlie, as it was known. Our platoon was undermanned, as many units in the military are. Due to the Army's inability to recruit men for the Infantry, we eventually deployed with thirty-three soldiers instead of the standard forty-two. Here we see the point of the 18X-ray program. You promise all these guys a Green Beret knowing many will fail, and when they do, you fill the ranks of the regular Army.

It's a pretty great idea, in my opinion, at least in theory. But all these dropouts in one place made this unit seem like the place where dreams go to die. I have never met a more morally defeated, self-deprecating group of men in my life. I fit right in, though, so I was by no means complaining.

It was just very evident that these men's motivations had been broken long before I had arrived at the unit. It wasn't that there were not good men or even good soldiers in the unit because there were and still are, but they didn't want to be there, and they showed it.

Once in Two Charlie, I was sent to a windowless office to meet my squad leader, Sergeant Hunter. As I entered the small room, he turned and looked at me with an inquisitive look on his face.

"Yes?" he said slowly.

"Uh, I'm Specialist Summerfield. I was told to come tell you I am in your squad now, Sergeant," I said nervously.

"Hmm…. Likely story," he said, slowly stroking a nonexistent beard.

After a short awkward silence, he said, "Welcome to Two Chuck. You're my new Bravo team leader. Go find Bertelli and Lemmon and introduce yourself. They are in your fire team."

With that, I made my way out the door behind me to find the two men who would make up my fire team. As I was exiting the office, it dawned on me that this man had just placed me in charge of other people. I had absolutely no qualifications to lead a fire team in combat, none whatsoever. I just so happened to have been promoted to Specialist right before coming to the unit, and that was all that I needed, apparently. I can remember thinking, "I'm not sure why, but all right, I guess."

I would later find out that Sergeant Hunter was an intelligent man who had spent several years working in the civilian world before joining the Army. He had a wealth of combat experience and kept the standard and his military bearing better than any other soldier that I would meet throughout my time in the Army. He was known for his ruthless demeanor, but I would say that he was almost always fair. He looked a lot like Judge Dredd, according to Lemmon, since he was always scowling and had a five-o'clock shadow by 0900 every morning. He would go on to be a great mentor to me, whether he knew it or not.

I may not have been qualified to be a team leader, but my fortune was not lost on me, since the men below me in position got physically destroyed anytime anything went wrong. This is supposed to create some sense of camaraderie, or the idea that everyone is in the fight together. Unfortunately, all it really does is create resentment toward leaders; to the point that soldiers did things like slash leaders' car tires and haze those who get everyone else in trouble. I endured a lot of the same nonsense, or what we called fuck-fuck games, but I was also shielded from some of it due to the fact that I was a team leader.

This was because each time that the squad leaders got done scuffing up all the lower enlisted, the team leaders would do it again. Given that I was a team leader, I got to skip one of the rounds of fuck-fuck games. As a consolation prize, I didn't scuff up the few people under me at the conclusion of round one.

On one occasion, our squad leaders made us do a myriad of stupid exercises because there were Chinese menus from a local restaurant scattered all over the barracks. Apparently, a nearby Chinese deliveryman had placed them in the doors of the barracks rooms and the wind had scattered them about while we were at work. When the squad leaders found out the barracks were littered, they had us doing pushups to the chants of "Chinese, if you prrease." Once the squad leaders had had their fun with us, the team leaders took over. The other team leaders decided to make the privates carry giant rocks up and down the hill outside, pretending like they were deliverymen with Chinese food. Every time the privates would get to the top of the hill, the team leaders would tell them they had got their order wrong and then send them back down the hill for a different rock. This was all done under the guise of instilling in the men the need for a clean barracks. Instead of joining in, I grabbed my guys and headed back to the barracks, where we picked up the menus and I called the Chinese restaurant. I asked the manager to please not leave menus at our building again, so as to save us a great deal of pain and suffering in the future. He politely agreed, knowing full well my troubles, since he had been in my unit years earlier.

I could have joined in, screamed, yelled, and made the privates do jumping jacks till they vomited. I just didn't have it in me. I hated getting scuffed up for stupid shit, so I wasn't going to do it to other people, at least not without good reason. Sometimes it is necessary, but for the most part, I just tried to do a good job and give no more grief than was necessary to get the job done. I would try to earn the men's respect through hard work and knowing my job, not by wielding arbitrary power that luck had bestowed upon me. There were always those team leaders who would, though.

One such individual, by the name of Sullivan, did just this, and was one of the worst soldiers I have ever met. He definitely looked the part of a soldier, even though he was the farthest thing from it. He was of average height but noticeably over-muscled and had full-sleeve tattoos on both arms. He played the part of the tough guy, but when push came to shove, he would always find a way out of the hard missions that the platoon would face on the future deployment. He would destroy privates for minor things like uniform violations, making them do hundreds of pushups for the most trivial of things. He would also ask them basic military questions and then scuff them up when they didn't know the answers. Most of the information he would ask them was of no real value, like how many buttons are on your uniform. To make things worse, Sullivan knew none of this information himself. He would use a cheat sheet to question them because he did not bother to have the information memorized. Given this soldier's performance, I knew no matter how bad I was at my job, if I didn't act like this piece of shit, I wouldn't be the worst team leader in the platoon. So I was starting this endeavor out on a positive note for a change.

A few weeks after settling into the unit, I came to realize that the men in the platoon were just back from their pre-deployment train-up in California. I was a little disappointed I had missed it; the deployment was fast approaching, and I would have liked the additional training. With this on my mind, one day at work I approached Lemmon, my rifleman. Lemmon was a taller guy with an athletic build who had his share of prison tattoos. He was noticeably from the South—Mississippi, to be exact—and spoke with a slow drawl even when everyone else was in a hurry. He cared little for what the Army wanted him to do and almost never got worried about anything. He also had a way of lounging around that was almost superhuman; he just seemed to melt into whatever surface he was lying on. He also embodied the saying, "Why stand when I can sit; why sit when I can lie down?" Nevertheless, he was a great soldier and perhaps had the best demeanor a lower enlisted man could have.

As I approached Lemmon to talk to him about the train-up, he was lying half in and half out of his locker, using his rucksack as a platform to extend the base of his locker into an almost proper bed.

"Hey, Lemmon, what all did you crazy kids learn in California?" I asked.

"Shit, man.... We didn't really learn much. Most of the time was spent sitting on this mountain seeing who could club the most rats to death," he replied, dragging his words.

"What?" I asked, somewhat confused.

As I was speaking to Lemmon, my M249 gunner, a pudgy kid named Bertelli who looked to be almost twelve years old, came over to the conversation. Bertelli was intelligent, more so than I, but incredibly immature, and he lacked the common courtesy that one should afford individuals in everyday life. I had a genuine dislike for the guy, but overall, we got along fine, and he was a good member of my team and a knowledgeable soldier.

"Yeah, yeah, we didn't learn shit, man," Bertelli said, as he barged into the conversation.

2. With No Training and Little Intel

"Nothing, huh?" I asked, shaking my head.

"Nope, we didn't learn anything. They just left us on a mountain to pull security and all we did was kill rats," Bertelli repeated.

Lemmon explained that everyone literally turned into savages. There were just thirty shirtless guys running around with clubs and cans of Rem Oil. Apparently, one guy would use the Rem Oil and a lighter like a flamethrower to burn the rats out from under rocks. Then, when they would scatter, everyone else would club the shit out of them as they tried to escape the fire. When the training cadre finally came to relieve them from the little outpost (OP), there were hundreds of dead rats hung on the razor wire surrounding the OP. I was relieved to know that I had not missed any valuable training, while at the same time distraught that they had not received any. All I could do was laugh at the ridiculousness of the whole thing.

One of the many instances that Lemmon could be found sleeping in his locker. On this particular occasion, he is using his rucksack as a blanket instead of a hide-a-bed (courtesy Norman Blackman).

We oftentimes see the rigors of training that highly dedicated and motivated soldiers go through in movies and on television. Prior to their deployments, we see them go through this amazing transformation and think that all of our service members are well trained. This is absolutely not the case for the enlisted men in the regular Army. At least, this was not my experience. We had no magical movie montage to whip us into shape.

Three days prior to our departure for Afghanistan, Sergeant Hunter called us together for a squad meeting. Finally, after months of having no idea what we were going to be doing down range, he had at last been briefed. As we all circled up around Sergeant Hunter, I can remember thinking, about damn time! Not that I blamed Sergeant Hunter, because our unit had kept us all in the dark. Honestly, our leadership was probably in the dark themselves up until this point.

The good news was that we were going to be dealing with a great deal of improvised explosive devices (IED). This was great, since we had absolutely zero training with IEDs. Further castigating our morale, Sergeant Hunter explained that the IEDs would be so numerous that what little conventional training we had done would be completely useless. Sergeant Hunter explained to us that conventional tactics would not work. The insurgents in the area had gotten used to them, and they employed IEDs extremely effectively to stop these maneuvers.

Conventionally, if a unit is fired on by the enemy, they would take cover, shoot back, establish a base of fire, fix the enemy in position, and then some part of the element would move to the vulnerable side of the enemy's position to finish them off. The insurgents got smart to these tactics and started planting IEDs in places that would provide us with good cover from rifle fire. Thus, when we took cover from their incoming fire, we would step on the IEDs. The insurgents also quite regularly placed IEDs in shady spots on patrol routes as well. So, if one tried to escape the brutal Afghan heat, he would again step on an IED. The insurgents would also try to predict which side of their ambush positions U.S. personnel would likely try to flank them on. They would then place IEDs so as to stop them from being able to approach their vulnerable side. This effectively reduced one's squad to single-file, extremely slow patrols with a minesweeper in the front to clear the path in order to provide the patrol with the only safe place to move. All of this meant that no one would under any circumstances leave the paths that had been cleared.

After his explanation, Sergeant Hunter left the floor open for any questions.

Lemmon, ever so slowly, raised his hand and asked, "So, who the fuck are we even fighting? The Taliban?"

"That's a good question, Lemmon," Sergeant Hunter said, shaking his head and laughing to himself. "Yes, technically we will be fighting the Taliban. We will be heading into the region of Afghanistan that is known as the birthplace of the Taliban. So they will likely be our most prevalent opposition. That said, you need to keep in mind that it is shades of guilt over there."

2. With No Training and Little Intel

"Shades of guilt, Sergeant?" Bertelli asked, somewhat perplexed.

"Yes, shades of guilt. Everyone you run into will be guilty in some way. They may not be a Taliban fighter, but they will be helping them in some capacity. They could be giving IED components to the Taliban or they could be hiding fighters in their homes. Little old ladies will be used as lookouts. These bastards will even strap a bomb to a little kid and send him running straight toward us."

"So we are fighting everyone, then," Bertelli presumed.

"Make no mistake, men, some of us are going to die. Take a look around this locker room. Some of these men will not be coming back," Sergeant Hunter said with a noticeable change in demeanor.

The next day we were called out to an open field next to our locker room. Here we were to receive the only block of hands-on IED instruction that I have ever been given. As I was standing there waiting for the class to begin, a young goofy-looking private whom I had never seen before stepped out front to give the class. He had never deployed, nor was he a member of an Explosive Ordnance Disposal (EOD) team. Upon starting his block of instruction, he was noticeably nervous and was quite unsure as to where he should begin. Once he finally began, we watched as he lazily buried a fake IED under some pine needles. Then proceeded to "find it" using a mine detector called the Mine Hound. Once he located it, he lay face-down on the ground and probed the needles with a knife so as to pinpoint its location. Then he "dug up" the IED and disposed of it. This block of instruction was no more than fifteen minutes long and in no way prepared us for what was to be our actual task in country.

As he concluded his demonstration, every one of us started asking him a myriad of questions. People wanted to know about snap-backs, pressure plates and booby traps. He had not one single answer to our laundry list of questions. To make matters worse, he explained that he didn't know anything about IEDs. The only reason he was there was that some sergeant had made him come down there and teach us the class. You could tell that Sergeant Hunter was thrilled by this answer as he stood there and scowled at the private until he slinked away.

Following that confidence-inspiring block of instruction, we rehearsed these techniques for a few short hours and packed away the minesweeping equipment, which was not to be seen again until we were in Afghanistan.

※ ※ ※

Just two days later, we boarded a plane that would eventually lead us to the Kandahar Province of Afghanistan. I have never been very fond of long plane rides, but no one on that plane was in a hurry to get to our destination. Once on the ground inside Kandahar Air Field, I grabbed my gear and circled up with the squad. The majority of us were surprised just how damn cold it was on the tarmac. The climate in Afghanistan, as we would all learn the hard way, is incredibly inhospitable. It's freezing cold in the winter and blazing hot in the summer.

Immediately after all men and equipment were accounted for, we prepared to go do some IED training lanes. Normally I am the first to complain about more useless training the Army is making me do. Not this time, though. The fact that we were to receive more instruction was reassuring. I was not overly confident in the knowledge that the confused private had bestowed upon us.

Once at the class, we were greeted by an actual IED expert. "What luck," I thought. "Perhaps this guy has actually seen an IED at some point in his life." We circled around the man and he started to ask us questions about IEDs. He wanted to know what we had been taught about their disposal, so he asked for someone to demonstrate the proper way to disarm an IED on his lanes.

Behind him, he had several rectangular training lanes roped off with engineer's tape. Inside those lanes, he had buried several mock IEDs that would buzz if set off. Following his request, two men approached the lanes and proceeded to show him what we knew how to do. When the men showed him their minesweeping techniques in combination with their knife-probing removal tactics, he laughed so hard he had to take a seat to catch his breath. Once he finally composed himself, he went on to tell us that many IEDs are booby-trapped so that they will go off if one tries to dig them up in this manner. Additionally, he stated that he had even seen some with magnetic triggering mechanisms that would detonate if touched with a metal object like a knife. He then told us that if we found an IED with the Mine Hound to cordon the area off and call EOD.

"There is a reason why there is an entire military occupational specialty devoted to IEDs!" he said, still laughing. "If need be, you guys can mark the IEDs and go around them to complete your mission. For example, if it is a time-sensitive matter. OK, then, are there any questions?" the IED expert said, still smirking and shaking his head.

"Is there such a thing as a snap-back IED?" Bertelli asked while raising his hand. We had heard about IEDs that one could step on but that would not explode until you stepped off them. They would effectively leave you trapped in place, like one would see in the movies.

Again, the man laughed as he replied, "There is no such thing as a snap-back IED. The stories that get back to the States are just ridiculous!"

Once our training was complete, we gathered our things and exited the training area the same way that we had entered. As I threw my rucksack over my shoulder and turned toward the exit, I could see a group of seven tactical vehicles waiting for us. Sergeant Hunter directed me to the vehicle at the front of the file.

First in the formation was a MATV, which is an up-armored vehicle that seats four, plus has a turret for a gunner. It has four doors, and one enters and exits it much like any normal everyday vehicle. This particular MATV was fitted with a mine roller since it was the first vehicle in the formation. The mine roller is a large steamroller-like front mount that extends some fifteen feet out in front of the vehicle it is attached to. Instead of one large wheel like a steamroller, it has several smaller wheels that are designed to detonate IEDs out in front of the vehicle. This is, of course, done in order to keep the occupants of the vehicle safe from the blast should they find an IED the wrong way.

Once we were loaded up, we headed to our combat outpost (COP), which was known as Nalgham. Our outpost was a little bit smaller than a football field and was surrounded by fifteen-foot Hesco walls. There were six guard towers spaced out equally around the perimeter. Each tower was built out of plywood and sandbags, and even had a roof on it to help with the elements. There was one entry control point (ECP) on the north side and a dismounted gate on the south side. We would also share the outpost with one platoon of soldiers from the Afghan National Army (ANA). Inside, we had three rows of four tents on the east side of the outpost, and the ANA had one row of four tents on the west side. In between two of the three rows of tents, there were bunkers built out of concrete barriers. These bunkers were to be used if we ever needed to take cover from incoming mortars. Just north of our bunkers was a small tent that we used as a chow hall and meeting area, and just north of the ANA tents there was a large area that we all used as a motor pool, in which both we and the ANA parked our vehicles. Once familiar with our living quarters and security positions, we settled into what would be our home for the next seven months.

– 3 –

Snap-Backs and Taliban?

The entirety of February at COP Nalgham was filled solely with mind-numbingly boring guard duty. Just hours upon hours of standing in the same place waiting for an enemy that would never come. I can remember thinking that if this was all we were going to do on this deployment, the Taliban wouldn't have to kill me because I would do it myself. The only thing I had to look forward to each day was going back to my tent and sleeping for a few hours before my next guard shift began.

The tents we lived in were simple one-room areas lined with ten Army cots on each side. This left just enough space down the middle for a narrow walkway. Most of the cots were covered with dusty old mattresses that had been left by the previous unit. They were actually pretty comfortable, and those who did not have them were a little jealous. It may not have been much, but it was all we had to look forward to.

After a long twelve hours of guard duty, I eagerly made my way to that Army cot. All I had to do was weave my way back through the motor pool toward our living area. Just as my tent was within sight, I saw Lemmon peeking out the door waiting for me. When he saw me, he called me inside with an excited wave of the hand. Following Lemmon inside, I heard Sergeant Hunter calling First Squad together for our mission briefing. I quickly set my gear down on the rickety shelf over my bed and thought, "No way are we actually going to leave this shithole of an outpost for a real mission." I can remember sitting down on Lemmon's bed while the rest of the guys in the team gathered round to get the brief from Sergeant Hunter. As he pulled out his map and began, I could tell that a lot of us cherries were in disbelief. We had done dozens of briefs just like this one in training, but this one was real. We would finally get to see what we could do in a real-world mission. No more

3. Snap-Backs and Taliban?

The tent that First Squad lived in when we were not out in the field doing continuous operations (courtesy Brandon Young).

blanks, no more pretend, it was time to actually push into the Talibros' backyard and say hi.

Sergeant Hunter explained that our goal was to build a road connecting our COP and Bravo Company's COP. This would give us the ability to conduct presence patrols in between the two COPs, reinforcing each other should we need help while at the same time limiting the Taliban's freedom of movement. Our part of the mission would be to take control of two defendable positions in the area so as to provide overwatch for First and Third Platoon, Charlie Company, who would be in charge of constructing the road.

Our element would consist of our platoon, an EOD team, a handful of ANA soldiers and Afghan Local Police Officers (ALP). We would all move out some eight kilometers to a large hill that would provide a good vantage point of the area. In between Nalgham and the hill there was a suspected IED belt estimated to be at least a kilometer long and five hundred meters wide. IED belts are large areas of land that are covered with large numbers of IEDs, which effectively turns them into active minefields.

"So, we literally have to cross a minefield in order to reach the hill, Sergeant?" I asked Sergeant Hunter as he pointed to its location on the map.

"Yes, but it gets better," Sergeant Hunter said, looking up at us from the map.

"I like better, Sergeant," Bertelli said sarcastically.

"I'm glad you do, Bertelli," Sergeant Hunter said as he pulled a piece of paper out of his shoulder pocket. "I have here some genius's idea of a packing list." He handed me the paper.

As I looked over the list of thirty-six bottles of water, hundreds of rounds of ammo, ten MREs, multiple pairs of pants, uniform tops, sandbags, and more, my expression grew noticeably less enthusiastic. Sergeant Hunter watched as I examined the list and he burst out laughing as my face contorted in disapproval. He knew it was a shitty list and was laughing half out of surprise and half out of frustration.

After Sergeant Hunter finished the brief, he told us to pack and clean our rifles, because we may actually get to use them the following day. Once I'd packed my rucksack, I tried to throw it over my shoulders like I would on any other day. I was met with a hilarious surprise, as the ruck was so heavy I had to have Lemmon help me put it on.

"How bad is it?" Sullivan asked me with a concerned look on his face.

"You know what? It is really not that bad once you get it on," I said sarcastically.

"Really?" he said with a look of relief on his face.

"No, not really! I can literally feel it rupturing the discs in my fucking spine, dude," I said almost madder at him than at the list.

The contents of the packing list weighed almost exactly 120 pounds. I know this because I weighed it on a little bathroom scale I found at the back of our tent. I only weighed it so I could add mental insult to physical injury. I wanted to accurately bitch about my 120-pound rucksack for the entire duration of the operation.

After we finished packing our rucks, Sergeant Hunter called us over to brief us on what to expect while working with the ANA and ALP. He wanted to make it clear that the ANA were complete fuck-ups. They had almost no training at all. They slept on guard duty. They constantly discharged their firearms accidentally and they endlessly consumed narcotics. That understood, their inability to do anything that even resembled a military operation was nothing compared to the ALP. These motherfuckers were made up of farmers, child soldiers, and Taliban fighters. Each of them was only there for a paycheck at best and to hurt U.S. military personnel at worst. Thus, he expected us to pay attention to what we were doing. He didn't want us to turn our backs on these guys because they would shoot us in it. With that useful piece of information, we all laid down and got a little rest before our first mission.

The following morning, we stepped off at 0600 on the dot. I use "stepped off" only in the loosest sense of the phrase because we looked pathetic. As we struggled to leave Nalgham, we looked like a bunch of newborn calves trying to walk for the first time in our miserable lives. Like most guys, I had set my ruck on the ground, climbed inside the shoulder straps, then tried to stand. As I violently struggled towards an upright position, I could see guys crawling on all fours while others used their rifles like crutches to stand. There were even some guys who needed the help of two other soldiers to get to their feet. I could feel my spine being destroyed under the weight of my rucksack. It was laughable to think that we could get into a firefight at some point in time during this patrol. We were all but combat ineffective before we even got out of the gate.

Just ten short minutes into the patrol, guys were starting to fall behind. I felt like I was carrying a refrigerator full of bricks on my back. When I turned to see how Bertelli was doing, he looked defeated. His M249 was dangling from his neck and both of his arms were draped over top of it. The weight of his ruck and the 1200 rounds of 5.56 he was carrying had cut off the blood flow to his arms, causing them to dangle uselessly in front of him. The platoon was literally falling apart within sight of the COP. Our leaders reluctantly came to the conclusion that we were not going to make it much further, which forced us to take a short halt at a local Afghan police station so that we could regroup. Once there, the leadership decided that we would take twenty of the thirty-six bottles of water out of our rucksacks, then place them in an ALP truck that would then follow us for the duration of the movement.

"Really? We are going to bring a truck with us? What a great idea," I said out loud. "Why don't we throw our rucksacks in the truck and then grab them when we get to our fucking destination?"

Just as I said this, our platoon sergeant (PSG) came around to the side of the truck I was standing on. He was an imposing figure at 6 feet and 240 pounds. He had the shortest fuse of anyone I had ever met. He was terrible with the guys' names and was never reasonable even on the simplest of matters. This build and demeanor gave him the appearance of a bulldog with a bad Army haircut.

"How do you know how to run an operation? Have you ever deployed before, Smithfield?" he yelled, throwing his twenty bottles into the back of the truck.

"Maybe not, but I'm also not a moron," I grumbled as I headed back to my place in the formation.

When I got there, Lemmon asked me, "Does he not know your name is Summerfield?"

"Fuck, no. He literally always gets it wrong. He called me Sammerson yesterday," I said as I shook my head.

"Sammerson." Lemmon laughed to himself.

So, much to my dismay, we continued on with our now only 100-pound rucksacks. They felt lighter for almost eight seconds, but then immediately became just short of unbearable once again. I have no doubt that if we had not dropped those twenty bottles, we would not have made it. Nevertheless, I do believe that this was as heavy as they could have been and still allow us to continue mission.

Shortly after we'd left the Afghan police station, we found our first IED of the deployment. It was so close to the police station entrance that some of the guys in the formation had not even left the checkpoint yet, which gives you just a glimpse into the incompetence of the ALP. Much to my surprise, it was one of the ALP officers who found it. After a moment of reflection, however, I decided that it was either by luck or because he had put it there himself. Regardless of how he found it, we were forced to take a short halt and wait for EOD to do their thing.

It took EOD around thirty minutes to complete their Blast in Place (BIP), which basically consists of locating and destroying the IED by way of a controlled detonation. Once EOD finished disposing of the IED, we were up and moving again, but not for long. We barely made it another fifty meters before we found our second IED. We took another short halt and the IED was disposed of in the same manner as the first. We continued this process for the next several hours, stopping every fifty to 100 meters and waiting for EOD to dispose of the IEDs. With each short halt, the weight of the rucksacks became more and more unbearable. During a short halt, soldiers take a knee and face outward to pull security. This allows one to reduce his silhouette while at the same time taking a short breather. It might have been the standard, but staying on one knee and holding that weight up proved to be quite exhausting. Given our pace and the way the men were starting to look, I asked if we could drop the rucksacks during the short halts.

"What's that, Sammysauce?" the PSG growled at me.

"Oh, I was just wondering if we should drop these rucks during these thirty-minute halts, Sergeant," I said, knowing full well what he was going to say.

"Take them off? What do you know about the Army? Leave them on, roger!" he said as he moved to the front of the file.

Deciding to just forget about the PSG, I turned toward my squad leader. "Hey, Sergeant Hunter, is it normal to find this many IEDs on a patrol?"

"Fuck no! I don't think we found this many IEDs on my entire last deployment!" he replied.

"Interesting," I thought as I switched knees and waited for another BIP to be completed. While I steadied myself on my fresh knee, I took a look around to see how the other guys were doing. I quickly realized that we all had become quite lazy and unprofessional. Most guys were now sitting down instead of taking a knee. There were even some who were on all fours waiting for EOD to finish their BIP. I can remember seeing one of the Assistant Gunners (AG) on his hands and knees, trembling under the weight of his rucksack. As one can imagine, this is by no means the aggressive and proactive security posture that one would want to adopt while on patrol in Afghanistan.

Shortly after midday, while my squad was the lead element in the file, the ALP found another IED. I could clearly see the IED's location just a few meters ahead of me. However, by this time in the day, finding an IED had lost all its excitement as the fatigue and monotony made me care little if the thing went off. While waiting for EOD to come to the front, I sat down next to Townsend, who was kneeling next to a small kalat wall. Townsend was a stocky man with a square jaw who had been a Marine prior to joining the Army. He was on his second deployment and seemed to have a good head on his shoulders. Townsend is one of those guys who always tried to do the right thing, and I was not surprised to find out he had been an Eagle Scout when he was a kid.

As Townsend and I sat there, the ALP officers became impatient waiting for the EOD team and decided to dig the IED up themselves. As they began carelessly probing the ground with a shovel, Townsend decided it would be smart to move back a safe distance away from the IED. Passing by, he tried to convince me to go back with him. I was having none of it, however, because I had finally gotten into a comfortable position. I was

Townsend on a presence patrol south of Nalgam. As always, he is just happy to be doing Army stuff (courtesy Brandon Young).

so tired I hoped it blew me up! In fact, I was so unconcerned with the matter I just sat there staring at the dirt in front of me. Besides, getting blown up had its advantages; I wouldn't have to carry this goddamn rucksack any farther.

Just as Townsend passed behind me, the ALP started shouting and screaming in Pashto. I looked up just in time to see an ALP officer throw his shovel in the air and sprint toward the open field next to us. As his shovel hit the ground, I noticed black smoke rolling out of the ground where the IED was located! I just looked at the smoke and thought, "Well, OK then." Turns out they had struck the pressure plate on the IED with the shovel and set it off. Only due to its faulty construction did the IED not go off like it was supposed to. After it sputtered out and all was declared well, the ALP guys regrouped, grabbed their shovel, and had a good laugh.

After the all-clear was given, Townsend passed back by me and took up his security position once again. He just stared at me in disbelief. He had decided that I was trying to be a hard-ass, but after seeing my reaction

3. Snap-Backs and Taliban?

The graveyard that our unit took over for joint operations with Bravo Company. We, of course, referred to it as Dick Mountain for the duration of the deployment (courtesy Brandon Young).

he was convinced I really didn't care what happened. Once you reach a certain level of fatigue, your priorities start to shift. I didn't have the energy to worry about IEDs anymore. I had to stare at that dirt in front of me.

After that professional IED disposal, we picked up and moved to within sight of the hill. The hill was about fifty meters high and about 100 meters across, with a giant dick-shaped termite mound sticking out of the east side of it. We would later come to realize the hill was actually a graveyard. It was covered with mound-shaped graves and multi-colored flags that marked them somewhat like gravestones.

Now that we had visual contact on the target, our forward observer (FO), Douglas, came up to the front of the file to call in air support. Douglas was of average height and build but was surprisingly athletic. He never seemed to get tired and he knew his job extremely well. This was his second deployment, and even though he was only a Specialist, he enjoyed a certain amount of autonomy that most specialists do not. This was due in part to his ability, experience, and athleticism. Douglas thought that the dick was such a noticeable landmark when he called for the Kiowas to scout the hill for enemy forces, he told them to call contact when they saw the dick.

Shortly after his call the radio crackled with, "We have contact on the dick. I say again, contact on the dick."

"Roger that, contact on the dick," Douglas said with a smile.

It was funny as hell, but I was too tired to laugh. Once the Kiowas called in with the all-clear, we moved the last few hundred meters to the foot of the hill. It had taken us nearly ten hours to move just eight kilometers. Ten hours under 100-pound rucksacks is always exhausting, but it was particularly painful for us considering that not once did we take those rucks off.

Now at the foot of the hill, my squad started to form a security perimeter around the base while Third Squad went to sweep it for IEDs. I started to feel like it was taking a really long time to clear the area when word had got back to me that McCance, a member of our company Intelligence Support Team (COIST), had stepped on a snap-back IED! This, of course, meant that he was now stuck in place!

"Holy fuck! Really?" I said as I looked over my shoulder trying to get a glimpse of what was going on.

Upon hearing me, Denton, one of our special kids, asked me. "What's wrong?"

"McCance stepped on a snap-back IED!" I said, still surprised.

"Nuh-uh, no way! The IED expert said that they weren't real!" Denton said in disbelief.

"Well, run up there and tell McCance that. I'm sure he will be glad to hear it!" Lemmon shouted over to Denton.

As McCance stood there motionless, those around him scrambled in an attempt to come up with a solution. Someone called for EOD while a few others just waited there motionless as if moving might somehow set it off. He could feel the pressure plate compressing precariously under his foot. As everyone stood there half-waiting and half-hoping, one of the ALP's child soldiers came up to examine the IED. Just as McCance was about to tell him to get back, the child grabbed a battery wire that was sticking out of the ground and yanked it out from underneath the pressure plate! After his heart skipped about twenty beats, McCance realized that the IED's battery had been disconnected, rendering it useless. It wasn't the best way to disarm an IED, but it worked and he was grateful.

Lemmon who was just a few feet from McCance when he stepped on the pressure plate, had been trying to pull security and listen to the chaos behind him. He said that he was trying to look for bad guys, listen to them, and figure out if it was going to explode and kill everyone all at the same time. I can remember the look on his face after it was all said and done. I could tell that he'd had enough for the day.

After our adventure with the snap-back IED, we left two squads and the ALP on the hill. Then my squad, a gun team, and the ANA moved on to our position in a nearby mud hut. Almost all Afghan mud huts are constructed in the same way. They have four ten-foot walls that form a rectangle creating a small courtyard. This courtyard can vary in size, but the average size is 100 by 200 feet. Inside the courtyard, they usually have one wall, with a few rooms built into it, which provides some refuge from the elements. As we entered the mud hut, our minesweepers started to check for IEDs while our ANA counterparts called their headquarters for supplies and stole items from nearby homes.

While the ANA were pillaging the local area, we set in security with one M249 covering the main road and three riflemen on the roof. I can remember watching the ANA conduct their business and being glad that we had left the ALP on Dick Mountain. The ANA and ALP could not be fully trusted, as their true intentions were hard to decipher. This was a lesson that would be taught again and again throughout my time in the Army. Bravo Company had just had two ANA soldiers attack them inside their COP a few weeks prior to this operation, which unfortunately resulted in the death of more than a few U.S. soldiers. I was glad, therefore, that the ALP and ANA had been separated between the two locations. I felt working with the two of them together had made the environment noticeably tenser.

* * *

All in all, the overwatch mission was quite boring, and despite the extreme cold, it was relatively easy. For some reason, there was no cold-weather gear or sleeping bags on the ridiculous packing list they had handed us the day before. Seeing that the temperature got down to as low as twenty-eight degrees some nights, we paid dearly for this oversight in the days to come. There was one man, however, in the entire platoon who had decided that, on top of all the shit that we had to bring, he would pack his windbreaker, fleece top and bottom. This man, of course, was our Eagle Scout Townsend.

Townsend, who was on the hill, woke up the first morning, put on his cold-weather gear, and made himself a cup of coffee. While everyone hunkered down in their ranger graves, he stood atop Dick Mountain comfortably sipping his coffee. I remember everyone telling me later that our PSG yelled at him for nearly thirty minutes because he should never have brought cold-weather gear, stating that it was too heavy, and the extra weight could have caused him to be a heat casualty the day before.

"You idiot, Townsend, are you trying to have a heat stroke? Are you trying to go down out here?" yelled the PSG.

"I'm fine, Sergeant," Townsend replied as the steam from his coffee wisped his cheeks.

"I thought you were tough. I thought you were a Marine, dammit!" yelled the PSG again.

"Being tough is fine, but being smart is better," thought Townsend as he warmed his hands on his canteen cup. It's also important to mention here that the PSG and the platoon leader (PL) had their sleeping bags brought out to them in a resupply the next day. They did not ask that any of our sleeping bags be brought out, just theirs.

The PSG's antics would have continued, but they were interrupted by a child screaming at the bottom of Dick Mountain. Two of the guys ran to the bottom of the hill to see what was going on, but did not find what they had expected. One of the ALP officers had pinned a local boy of about twelve years of age to the ground. The ALP officer had his pants down around his ankles and was clearly trying to force himself on the boy. The two U.S. soldiers broke them up and the boy ran back to a nearby village, never to be seen again.

The ALP officer was noticeably angry with the two soldiers. Surprisingly, it seemed as if he was angrier he had been stopped than ashamed of what he had been caught doing. Most of the guys were pretty shocked by this act, but we would come to find out over the course of the deployment that this was commonplace in this country, and in many cases leads to the death of the child.

* * *

Despite the regular Army nonsense and our Afghan counterparts' antics, the mission went smoothly—until we all started to get dysentery. The mud hut that we were staying in had three small rooms, one of which Sergeant Hunter, Lemmon, myself and a few others all slept in. Several of the guys had taken to sleeping two to a body bag in order to generate some body heat. And I mean literally a body bag: they had been brought in just in case we needed them. I, however, chose to sit in the corner alone and freeze all night, every night. I did this as opposed to sleeping in a body bag with a dude who had not showered for a month.

One night while I was freezing in my corner, someone jumped up on all fours and started frantically digging in his ruck. After my eyes focused in on who it was, I realized Sergeant Hunter was on his hands and knees with his pants down around his thighs.

"Great! Just great! I fucking shit my pants," he fumed in a whisper.

He was a pretty intense guy, but it was funny to see him in this state. As he was digging in his ruck, I realized he must be searching for something to clean himself with. So I pulled my baby wipes out of the top of my rucksack and threw them over toward him. As he struggled to find the best position from which to attack the puddle of filth in his pants, his main concern was actually my baby wipes. He wanted me to be absolutely sure that he could use them to clean up his mess. My squad leader was an actual leader and always put his men first, even when it came to trivial things like baby wipes, which he knew were a luxury in the field. While he was cleaning himself up, I realized that it was almost time for Lemmon and me to go on guard.

I woke up Lemmon, and we threw on our kits and climbed on top of the mud hut so as to assume our positions on the west side of the roof. As we moved into position, we passed by our ANA counterpart, who was supposed to be on guard duty on the east side of the roof. He was fast asleep on the ground, using a rocket-propelled grenade (RPG) as a pillow. He looked all too comfortable wrapped up ever so tightly in his cozy-looking sleeping bag.

"Poor little guy's all tuckered out," Lemmon said as he passed by.

"Fuck this guy," I laughed, stepping around him.

Despite Lemmon's comedic overtone, he was not feeling much better than Sergeant Hunter. As he settled into his position, he started to wrap himself in his poncho in a feeble attempt to stay warm. The wind was forcing that twenty-eight-degree weather to our very bones. After a few minutes of trembling, I looked over at Lemmon to see how bad he was suffering. He had wrapped himself in a cocoon that encapsulated his entire body. The only thing that was sticking out of that poncho was his green night-vision monocular, which was trembling violently as he scanned his security sector left to right. About an hour into the shift, I was starting to feel pretty sorry for myself. As I stood there complaining, Lemmon started to frantically attempt to escape his cocoon. Standing there staring at him, I tried to comprehend why he was desperately trying to shed his only source of warmth. Just as I decided to reach over and help, he vomited into his poncho! Failing to get out of his cocoon in time, he just slowly composed himself and sat back down. He then gracefully lounged into the side of the kalat wall that surrounded the roof, at which time he proceeded to cuddle up in the warmth of the vomit that had run down in between his armor and his uniform top. You know that you are having a good evening when the guy warming himself in his own vomit is making you jealous. "I would have been willing to put up with the smell for a little bit of warmth," I thought.

Unfortunately, Lemmon's comfort would not last, as he vomited some twenty more times on our two-hour shift. He did, however, manage to get his poncho off so that he could vomit over the side of the building the next time. This ruckus did manage to wake up our ANA friend asleep on the RPG, although all he did was move his sleeping pad further away from the sick guy vomiting and go back to dreamland. It was by no means ideal, but it seemed like progress of a sort.

Once our shift finally ended, I told Lemmon to go back to our room and I went to get our medic. Doc Gio was a tall guy who lived to do Cross-Fit and be a medic. He was super fit and carried way more gear than anyone else did on every patrol. He was a super-knowledgeable guy with a funny demeanor, which suited his profession perfectly. He always had a way of looking at the bright side of the Army, which was something that I never was able to do.

When I woke up Doc, he got right up, grabbed his aid bag, and went to help Lemmon. As Doc and I headed to our room, we realized that Lemmon had not just vomited twenty times, but he had vomited twenty times on the ANA's water supply. The ANA had stored their bottles on the ground directly below Lemmon's security position. I considered telling the ANA about the contaminated water but considering their help with security, I never did. The crazy thing, however, is that they drank every damn bottle of water Lemmon threw up on and not one of them got sick.

The next morning when supplies came in, Lemmon and Sergeant Hunter were sent back to Nalgham on our brand-new road. As we loaded them up on the supply trucks, I was starting to feel bad myself, but knew I only had to last two more days till we would all be picked up and taken back to our outpost. The next two days, however, were quite long as I was having the same problems that both Sergeant Hunter and Lemmon had been having. Each passing night, I felt weaker and weaker, which made the cold even more unbearable. I would sit in my little corner wrapped in a thin plastic poncho trembling violently. This routine was only interrupted by the constant diarrhea, vomiting, and guard shifts that made up my days.

On the final night of the mission, the Platoon Leader (PL) came in to check on me, since he had heard I was quite ill. The PL was by far the tallest man in the platoon. He had previously been a noncommissioned officer prior to becoming an officer, so he knew what it was like to be enlisted. He was intelligent and a quick thinker, and we were lucky to have him as a PL. When one speaks of "command presence during engagements," he could easily be the poster child: on more than one occasion, I witnessed him giving orders under fire standing fully erect while other men hunkered down behind cover. Once he saw the pitiful state of my existence, he went and grabbed several heating pads and draped them over my back. Seeing as I had no cold-weather gear, this was the first time I had been warm in ten days. It was a small gesture, but two hours of warmth after freezing for ten days is quite an experience, I can tell you that.

The next morning, we all packed up and prepared to head back to

3. Snap-Backs and Taliban?

Dick Mountain. Once there we would meet up with the transport vehicles that were to take us back to COP Nalgham. It was a short 400-meter movement, but I was weak, and that 100-pound ruck seemed to weigh 1,000 pounds at this point. Despite my fatigue, we made it back to Dick Mountain in one piece. Once there, Doc Gio had me and the other sick guys lie down off to the side of the dick-shaped termite mound, where he proceeded to give each of us one last IV before the trucks arrived. I just laid in the dirt on the edge of the mountain, staring at the sky, waiting for death. Most of us had been vomiting and had had diarrhea for several days now, and we were all very dehydrated. As Doc was hooking me up with an IV, the PSG came over to us with his usual caveman walk and angry scowl. I thought that he had come over to see how we were doing, but of course I was sadly mistaken. Once he reached our position, he just threw a single-blade dollar-store razor at each of us. Come to find out, someone above him in the chain of command had decided that no man would go back to the COP without a fresh shave. He just tossed me—a twenty-eight-year-old man with an IV in his arm and a ten-day beard—a single-blade razor from the dollar store to dry shave with.

He looked me right in the face and said, "You won't leave here till you shave, Sonderson!"

As he walked away, I thought, "What a piece of shit. First of all, there is not even a Sonderson in this fucking company, let alone the platoon. And second, why don't we all just shave when we get back to the COP, where there is water and shaving cream?" I grabbed the razor, looked at it like it owed me money then, smacked myself in the face with it three times, and let it fall to the ground beside me. I had resigned myself to either leave unshaven or die in place, because a dry shave just wasn't in the cards for me that day. Needless to say, when the trucks arrived, they let me get on and go back to COP Nalgham.

– 4 –

Farming for Taliban

A few weeks after our excursion to Dick Mountain, we took over a small abandoned compound that had been bombed way before my time in country. It had three remaining walls with three small rooms on one side and a large grape-drying hut attached to the opposite end. There was rubble scattered about, and someone could have easily hidden an IED of some kind in the compound. Given this possibility, before entering the building we had a team of security personnel and a minesweeper go in to clear it. As they went in, the ANA followed right behind. They scoured every corner, flipping over pots and pans searching for firewood, while others flopped down lackadaisically with total disregard for potential IEDs. We tried to convince them that this was dangerous, that if they would just give us a few minutes we would clear the area and they could set up camp. They just laughed in our faces and waved their hands in dismissal with the same quasi-feminine hand gesture they always use to dismiss things.

In the previous three days, we had found ten IEDs in the surrounding area and we were operating near an IED belt. This was of little concern to them; they just wanted to sit down, start a fire, and get high. In the infantry, you never start a fire in the field under any circumstances, because it gives away your position to the enemy. We had lost this battle days earlier, though, as they would throw ridiculous fits if we tried to stop them. So we came to a compromise: we would let them start a fire only during the day. While we were trying to convince the ANA how important minesweeping was prior to entry, the minesweeper found something.

Pulling the Mine Hound operator back from the potential IED, Sergeant Hunter called for EOD to inspect the area. Hearing the call from inside the compound, Staff Sergeant King made his way to the potential

4. Farming for Taliban

IED. Being the EOD team leader meant that this was by no means his first rodeo. He always had a calm demeanor and he worked slowly to ensure that he made no mistakes. Staff Sergeant King checked the ground, the wall and the surrounding area meticulously to verify the sweeper's finding. Shortly after he had begun, Staff Sergeant King sent Bertelli to go get the rest of the EOD team. This could only mean one thing: there was indeed an IED in the compound. While we waited for Bertelli to return, Staff Sergeant King explained that someone had placed a Chinese rocket in the wall and attached it to a pressure plate.

For some reason, we thought that this would impress upon the ANA the importance of sweeping prior to entry. Much to the contrary, they were quite unimpressed, and they barely looked up from where they were lying down and smoking weed. Nevertheless, all U.S. personnel moved out of the compound so EOD could dispose of the IED.

Once they had completed the BIP, I ran to the front of the file and headed to the entrance of the building to do the usual headcount as all soldiers ran past me into the compound and took up security positions. Bertelli's pudgy ass ran past me first, with his 1,200 rounds of M249 ammunition flopping from side to side working only to accentuate his feminine curves.

"One," I said out loud.

Next Sergeant Hunter ran past, frowning hard and glaring harder.

"Two."

Followed by Townsend with his usual smile and noticeably upbeat attitude.

"Three," I smiled, shaking my head.

As I turned my attention from Townsend to the next man, Lemmon, I noticed something attached to his kit that was swinging back and forth violently as he ran. "That's not a grenade, is it?" I thought. As he passed by, I realized that not only was it definitely a grenade, but it was a grenade that had two of the three safety mechanisms missing on it! To make matters worse, it was hung by the spoon in the Molle webbing of his kit! I lost count at four and just nodded as the rest of the platoon passed by. I turned into the compound, gave the all-clear, and headed straight to where Lemmon was inside the mud hut.

"Is there a reason why you are carrying that grenade like that, fella?" I asked as I pointed at his kit.

"What, this?" he said as he lazily smacked the grenade.

As I nodded, he continued, "Well, I saw the PSG carrying his grenade like this, so I figured it was OK."

"Yeah, yeah, he does do that," I said quietly. "But you do realize that his grenade has all the safeties on it, right?"

"Yeah, it probably does," Lemmon said in a matter-of-fact tone.

"You do also realize that the PSG is carrying a smoke grenade on his kit like that, as well, right?" I asked, expecting some kind of reaction.

"Now that you mention it, yeah, you're right. It is a smoke grenade. Purple, I believe it to be," Lemmon said with a smile.

"OK, well, let's put our grenade somewhere safer then, all right?" I said, laughing.

While Lemmon and I were sorting out the finer points of grenade stowage, we heard the ANA start arguing with Sergeant Hunter. Hunter wanted one person in each corner of the compound, three U.S. soldiers and one ANA soldier. The ANA were arguing that they could not spare the man, that they were too overworked, and it would be too difficult on their sleep cycles. Keeping in mind that they had seven soldiers, this seemed to be a flawed argument. They eventually agreed to pull security in the position next to where they had set up camp. That way they could all chat while on guard.

After the squabble, some of us started to fill sandbags so that we could fortify our security positions, while others went out and set up some claymore mines. After about thirty minutes of work, Lemmon realized that the ANA had no one in their designated security position.

"Hey, where the fuck is this ANA asshole who's supposed to be pulling security on the east side?" he asked, noticeably angry.

"Fuck? Of course, he's not there," I said.

Sergeant Hunter overheard us and asked the interpreter to go tell the ANA officer that we needed someone in that position right now. After talking to the interpreter for a few minutes, he looked over at Sergeant Hunter and just dismissively waved in his direction, clearly in no hurry to do anything.

Upon seeing this, Sergeant Hunter shook his head and said to himself, "Oh, OK, fuck me, huh? OK then, fuck me!"

He then went straight over to the ANA commander in order to explain the subtle intricacies of 360-degree security. This quickly escalated into everyone in the compound at each other's throats exchanging slurs and insults, none of which the opposing side could understand. Seeing the problem was not going to resolve itself, the PL finally came over and broke up the bickering. He then convinced the ANA to get into position while we went back to filling sandbags. Prior to leaving for this mission, the PL had hoped that the ANA would help fill sandbags and pull security when

4. Farming for Taliban

Lemmon sitting in his fighting position (ranger grave) in the graveyard (courtesy Brandon Young).

we got to the compound. That hope faded quite rapidly, since we could barely keep them in a security position, let alone get them to do any manual labor. He had these hopes even though Sergeant Hunter said we would be lucky if they didn't shoot one of us in the back before we left.

The ANA soldier that they eventually got into the security position was doing it all kinds of wrong. He was pulling security facing inside the compound toward his ANA comrades, shooting the breeze. He didn't even have a rifle, since he had left it on the ground where he had previously been lying. This, of course, provides no more security than if he wasn't even in position. All these problems aside, the ANA felt like they were fulfilling their part of the bargain. There was someone technically in position. It is hard to imagine the disparities between a U.S. soldier and an Afghan soldier until you witness this spectacle in action. This spectacle was in full swing during this operation.

After we had filled a few hundred sandbags, the ANA got up from their campfire chat and started taking the sandbags we had filled. They just started removing them from the defensive position we had built around the M240B. They then started to construct a throne in their security position. They wanted to have somewhere comfortable to sit during their tireless guard shifts. Everyone, of course, got super pissed off by this. We promptly went over and took all the sandbags back, then told them if they wanted to build a fucking chair, they could fill their own sandbags. So they did just that! They filled exactly enough sandbags to build a chair, then they went back to lying around their campfire. The funny thing was they built the chair facing the wrong direction, toward the inside of the compound. They did this so that they could sit comfortably while they chatted with their friends. This position left their head and shoulders completely exposed to those outside the compound. It was crazy how terrible at being soldiers these guys really were. Sergeant Hunter and the PL decided that they would think of him as an early warning system. If he got shot in the head and fell into the compound, we would know to send one of our guys over to return fire.

As night approached, a truck with supplies pulled up for the ANA soldiers. They brought several things like buckets, pots, and even a dirty old mattress. I had thought that the mattress would be placed in one of the rooms so that they could sleep on it. This was only half true, since they immediately started to pull it up onto the roof so that they could sleep on it during their guard shifts. Just when I thought that the chair they built was ridiculous, they had to go and impress the hell out of me.

Apparently, they had decided that since they could not get out of pulling security, they would sleep while they were on guard. They had devised this ingenious strategy so as not to waste their time sleeping during the day when they could be doing drugs and playing grab-ass with one another. Some of them would actually wait till they were on guard to sleep, and when they were approached about this, they could not differentiate between being physically on guard and actually pulling security. The ANA had absolutely zero discipline and were completely devoid of the ability to look toward the future in a meaningful or productive manner. These security indiscretions would go on to be devastating in many scenarios throughout the deployment, and no amount of death ever shocked the ANA or ALP into improving efforts to maintain a security presence.

* * *

After a few nights of nothing, Sergeant Young noticed a light moving a few hundred meters off in the distance at around 0300. Sergeant Young was a stocky man with a solid build, and he had the squarest jaw I have ever seen. This thing was straight out of a Superman comic book. He had

4. Farming for Taliban

Sergeant Hunter resting just before we all had a discussion with the ANA about the subtle intricacies of 360 security (courtesy Brandon Young).

an incredibly composed demeanor, plus a wealth of combat experience, and was a great addition to our squad—so much so that even Sergeant Hunter pointed this out on several occasions.

"Hey, guys, you see that light?" Sergeant Young said while pointing to the east side of the compound.

"Where?" asked the PL as he stood up to get a better look.

"Holy shit! There is another light moving to link up with the first light," Sergeant Young added.

As I scanned the dark open farmland in front of me, I saw two lights that appeared to be headed straight for one another.

"It looks like two guys are headed to meet up, to me," I said.

"I bet they are just farming," someone said from the darkness on top of the roof behind me.

"Yeah, I'm sure that they are just farming, you stupid moron," yelled Bertelli from the other side of the compound.

"They are fucking Taliban performing a link-up, probably planning to attack our position," someone else added from the darkness.

"You want me to call in some 120mm mortars on top of them, sir?" asked the FO as he stepped up beside the PL on a small mound of rubble that allowed them to see over the kalat wall.

"No, no! Let's figure out who they are before we blow them up," replied the PL, noticeably taken aback by the hastiness of the idea.

"I'm here if you need me," said the FO with a chuckle.

"You can call in some loom rounds so that we can see what the fuck they are doing," the PL told him.

"Yeah, light those Taliban fucks up so that we can dome piece those sumbitches!" yelled another person in the obscurity of the night.

While the FO made his request for loom rounds, we all waited and watched, hoping to decipher the intentions of these two ominous lights. They were the only lights that we could see for miles, just floating menacingly in the total darkness of a moonless night. A few minutes after the FO's request, the radio crackled with a no-go on loom rounds. The PL was completely surprised that they wouldn't even grant us loom rounds. Higher command had decided that they were too dangerous. They feared that the shell casings may land on some poor civilians. The FO was noticeably saddened by the denial. He could now do nothing but sit back and watch.

So, with the loom rounds denied, the PL decided that he would have some of the M203 gunners or grenadiers shoot star clusters out into the field. They would not light the sky up like loom rounds, but we could get a better look at what was going on. Immediately following the order, Sergeant Young loaded one into the tube of his M203. With the weapon's iconic "thud" he then sent the round flying in the direction of the two lights. Once the illumination round reached its target, it exploded, lighting up the sky. As the star cluster rained down streams of light, the two lamps gave way to two human silhouettes. Due to the surprise of incoming fire, the two human figures hit the ground as a second explosion rang out over their heads.

"Roadhouse!" yelled Sergeant Young as he fired a third star cluster.

"Oh yeah, they are definitely Taliban fucks. Did you see how they hit the ground when that round went off?" yelled Bertelli.

"Definitely Taliban!" the FO added.

Even the interpreter joined in, stating, "Yes, they must be Taliban, as you say!"

Everyone was so certain that we were looking at the Taliban in action. This was one of our first missions, so most of us had no idea what we were doing. With this new-found piece of incriminating evidence, the FO was able to get authorization for some loom rounds, and they lit up the sky like it was daytime. The two men in the field were now low crawling in all directions, frantically trying to figure out what they should do to save their lives. The men finally chose a direction and ran as fast as they could off into the distance. With their escape into the night, the excitement started to dwindle, and the night eventually faded into day.

The next morning around 0600, three farmers came up to our security position and started screaming at Sanders, who was on guard at the time. Sanders had dropped out of Special Forces the exact same day as me, so I knew him fairly well by this time. He was a shorter guy with a quick wit and a deep-seated hatred for the Army. He was a good soldier, but the morose nature of his demeanor came out in a never-ending stream of hilarious insults and sarcastic comments. He was Native American by descent, but the PSG thought he was Mexican and always referred to him as Sanchez. As they were screaming at Sanders, he started nodding like he understood what they were saying in Pashto.

He just kept on nodding and replying in English with off-the-wall statements that had nothing to do with what they were talking about. At one point he even started giving them directions to a make-believe Burger King that he claimed was in the area. Sanders was pointing at random stuff in the distance and patting one of them on the shoulder while he spoke. He was so convincing for a moment the leader of the group looked as if he thought Sanders was actually trying to help him. After he had had enough fun with the three men, he finally called for an interpreter to come and see what they actually wanted.

Once the interpreter finally got out there, the men started to explain that they were the men from the night before and they were quite angry that we had shot at them. Turns out they were farming, and that they always farmed at night. Upon hearing this, some of the men yelled that they had to be lying and that no one farms at night.

"Bullshit! Who farms at night?" yelled Bertelli, while others agreed with him.

"Likely story!" someone else yelled, agreeing with Bertelli.

"Oh yes, it is very common for those low in stature to farm at night. This is the case as there is only one well in the village and the farmers have to share it," the interpreter explained.

"Why didn't you tell us this last night?" asked the PL, confounded by the terp's response.

"Oh, you guys said that they were Taliban, so I believed you," replied the interpreter.

"Holy shit, bro! You knew all this time?" Sanders laughed while patting the interpreter on the back.

This was a problem that we ran into often with our interpreters. They would literally believe anything that anyone said. If a man said that he was not Taliban, the interpreter would not only believe him but vouch for him. It did not matter if we caught the guy red-handed planting an IED. The interpreter would go so far as to argue his case for being innocent. It was a really interesting dynamic that we came across time and again. I had heard from some older soldiers that it was better to do this than to call someone a liar within the culture. I am unsure of the validity of this rationale. Nevertheless, it caused us more than a few headaches.

– 5 –

IEDs for Sale or Trade

When we were not on an adventure, the day-to-day grind that comprised most of the deployment dragged on. Most of our days were spent on guard duty or conducting presence patrols. We did two types of patrols: those that were on foot, or what we called dismounted; and those that required vehicles, or mounted. Our platoon did three daytime patrols and one nighttime mounted patrol every twenty-four hours. This on top of two six-hour guard shifts a day made for about four hours of free time every twenty-four hours. This was our allotted time for sleep, hygiene, letter writing, and Internet time. I use the term hygiene lightly as we had no showers at Nalgham and everyone smelled hilariously bad. The pace of the busy days made the time fly, and the seven-month deployment was moving along quickly. I will be forever grateful I joined the Army after they stopped doing twelve- and fifteen-month deployments.

Since I was a team leader, I spent most of my guard shifts at the gate of the COP, or what we called the entry control point (ECP). The ECP was constructed out of Hesco walls, sandbags, and plywood. It was shaped like a dugout that was about ten feet long by fifteen feet wide. Built into the front, there was a window designed so that we could shoot out of it if the need ever arose. This little area somewhat resembled a guard shack next to any other entry road one may see in the United States, just much more field expedient. Time at the ECP was spent letting patrols go in and out and dealing with ALP members who came to the gate looking for supplies like ammo or fuel.

The ECP guards were also partially responsible for handling a curious little program that I never really understood. This program was set up by the unit that we replaced, but we continued to do it. The program allowed the local ALP members to trade in IEDs they found for cash money. In theory, one could see how this might seem like a good idea, since it could help remove IEDs from the area and we would not have to find them ourselves.

There were a few problems with the program, however. First, we would pay them more for each IED than it cost to make five IEDs, so this program turned into a job opportunity for the locals. They would just make IEDs, bring them in for the reward money, and then use the money to buy the supplies to make more IEDs. They would claim that they dug the IED up on this route or that one, but the IEDs were all made of brand-new materials and clearly had never been buried anywhere. On top of that, we still found a metric shit-ton of IEDs on almost every patrol we went on. So, in my mind, we were just funding the Taliban. I brought up this issue in one of our platoon meetings but was promptly told I was just a stupid fucking team leader and that I knew absolutely nothing, so I left the issue alone. Needless to say, we continued the program for the majority of the deployment.

One day, Townsend and I had been stuck at the ECP for around fourteen hours. The men who were to replace us had run into some problems on patrol, and there was no one at Nalgham who could do it, since everyone was either on guard or slated to go on patrol. It was midday when we got the news that we would not be replaced for some time, and the Afghan heat in the beginning of April was starting to become quite unforgiving. As Townsend and I sulked around sweating and wishing for death, the radio crackled and broke the silence.

"ECP, this is SOG. Over." Sergeant Hunter was the sergeant of the guard.

Townsend grabbed the radio and said, "Send it, SOG."

"I need to know if echo sierra is down at the ECP. Over," the radio crackled.

"Echo sierra?" Townsend said to me with a confused look on his face. "That must be some kind of code, but how are we supposed to know what that means? This SOG is a fucking idiot. He must be sooo stupid."

"Those are my initials," I told Townsend with a sullen look on my face.

"Ohhh... OK. Never mind. I'm the idiot." Then Townsend replied into the radio, "Roger. He is down here, over."

"OK. Roger. Does he still have the tango victors on his person, over?" asked the SOG.

"Yes," I said.

"Roger. He does, over," said Townsend.

"OK. Tell him to pass those off to 2–2 [second squad leader] when his squad comes to the ECP to step off, over," said the SOG.

"Roger," Townsend said to the SOG while turning back toward me. "Tango victors?" he asked.

"Thermal vision goggles," I replied as I pulled them out of a pouch on my hip.

A few short minutes later, Second Squad made their way to the ECP to prepare for their presence patrol. All members of the squad were in full kit, head to toe, ready for battle, except for Swoyer. Swoyer, or the duck-billed battle puss as we sometimes referred to him, was one of the guys in our platoon who could never catch a break. He was short, unathletic, and not destined to be a leader—at least not in this man's Army. He walked and ran bow-legged like a cowboy and was often times the butt of the joke. Not to be too disparaging, I should add that he was genuinely a good person and helped me and every other member of the platoon more than he should have for how he was treated. He even saved the day on a few occasions. Second Squad moved in ready for war as the battle puss came waddling in after his squad members. In his arms, he was cradling all his gear like it was a baby octopus. There were cables and muzzles flailing in every direction. His team leader Sanders could not believe that he still didn't have one single piece of his equipment on. So, just like the Army had taught him, Sanders utilized a barrage of insults and threats to motivate him into action. You could tell by the look on Swoyer's face he was just moments away from buckling under the pressure of dressing himself.

While the PSG gave the mission brief, Swoyer furiously tried to reassemble his body armor. All of the body armor that we wore had a cable that ran through the different pieces so that one could pull a ripcord and it would fall apart and off his body. This was to aid one if he were ever stuck in a wrecked vehicle or fell into water. Well, Swoyer had accidentally pulled the ripcord on his vest, and now had no idea as to how to put it back together. He looked like a blind man trying to knit with his feet. He was just jabbing random cables into every crevice of the armor, hoping that it would make sense of itself in the end. After three times as long as it should have taken any other person, Swoyer closed the panel on the back of the vest and threw the armor on over his head. He then placed his hands on his hips triumphantly, celebrating his accomplishment. No sooner had his hands hit his hips than the vest broke in two, falling off him from his front and back. Everyone burst out laughing while the PSG screamed at him for being an idiot. Swoyer just scrambled back to work, rerouting the cable even faster than before! He had at most five minutes to get his entire kit on and he knew it.

Since he was working under the pressure of a time hack, he was able to get the job done in half the time. He stood up, and with a violent swing of the vest, he threw it angrily over his head. This time, however, the vest broke in two mid-swing, and the front half of the armor flew off and hit Sanders in the shin. Infuriated by Swoyer's incompetence, Sanders just stared at his shin in amazement.

Everyone was dying of laughter at this point, except for the PSG and Sanders of course. This second failure prompted Harris, our platoon designated marksman (DM), to run over to aid in the reassembly. Harris was of average build, carried himself well, and was extremely polite. He was a God-fearing man who held a prayer before each patrol and Bible classes when there was time. As Harris knelt down to help, the PSG gave the signal to move out. They had no option but to secure his kit on him en route. So that's what they did. As Swoyer walked, Sanders held the armor and Harris routed the cables. They were still fixing his kit when they rounded the corner of the COP out of my field of view.

After the Swoyer show came to an end, Townsend and I continued to hopelessly wait for someone to come and relieve us. While staring off into the nothingness of Afghanistan, the SOG came down to check on us. Like a good SOG, he had brought us some food, knowing that we had not eaten for several hours. As we were sitting there talking, a mounted patrol returned for the evening. We had no gate, so the entrance of the COP was blocked by a MaxxPro. The MaxxPro is an up-armored troop carrier and can transport up to seven people, depending on its design. It is built with a V-shaped hull that is designed to deflect an IED blast away from those inside it. MaxxPros have a rear ramp that allows four dismounted troops to enter and exit. There is a driver and passenger seat in front and a turret for the gunner. We had to back this big-ass truck up to let patrols come in and go out. This was normally a simple task, but some troops had a harder time than others, and Townsend was one of these troops.

With the mounted patrol waiting outside, Townsend jumped in the MaxxPro, slammed the vehicle in drive, and floored it, ramming the huge truck straight into the wall.

"Well, that's one way to do it," said Sergeant Hunter, frowning.

"Well, they won't make the turn in that way. He will have to back it up," I said

So, I started waving for Townsend to back the truck up, which he did with the same amount of zeal. Placing the truck into reverse, he rammed it straight into the wall on the opposite side of the entrance.

"Holy shit! He is talented!" Sergeant Hunter said, starting to get impatient.

After the patrol had all pulled inside, I ran over to the driver's side door to see if Townsend wanted me to move the truck back. But before I opened the door, Sergeant Hunter stopped me. He wanted to leave this up to Townsend and see how it played out. While we watched and hoped, Townsend placed the truck back in drive and rammed it into the wall one more time for good measure before he finally got it back into a good position.

"Holy shit, Big Town Diddy!" Sergeant Hunter said as Townsend jumped down from the truck. "That was some smooth driving."

"Thanks, Sergeant," Townsend replied, knowing full well it wasn't a compliment.

With that, Sergeant Hunter bid us au revoir and headed back to finish his SOG shift while Townsend and I waited yet several more hours before being relieved from our post.

– 6 –

Kotizi

Our next big mission came midway through April and was another joint operation with Bravo Company. We were to push into a village named Kotizi just northeast of our COP in order to secure an overwatch position to facilitate Bravo Company's movements farther north. For this mission, our element consisted of First Squad, one weapons team, a mortar team, a three-man scout sniper team, and a handful of ANA soldiers.

Prior to our mission brief, I'd had the foolish belief that we had learned our lesson with regards to carrying too much equipment, but I was sadly mistaken. We actually took more equipment than we had on the last big push. I made some futile objections but was informed that I had no military experience and that my existence was of little merit. My ridiculous packing list consisted of thirty-six bottles of water, twelve M4 magazines, forty 40mm, multiple THOR batteries, twenty sandbags, two flex linear door charges, two mortar rounds, a CamelBak, two-quart canteen, hooligan tool for breaching, and an assortment of uniforms, socks, ponchos, and other miscellaneous items. All equipment in total was well over 120 pounds this time, and we would pay for it dearly in the days to come.

Once I came to terms with the packing list, I learned that the mission plan dictated that we were to be transported to a local ANA base about four kilometers from our final objective. We would stay the night there and move out first thing in the morning. We were planning to step off right at sunrise so as to avoid the heat. It was April now and the heat at midday was actually quite brutal in the southern part of Afghanistan. Once we arrived at the ANA outpost, we did some last-minute gear checks, then prepared to rack out and get some rest.

I was the last soldier on guard duty inside the ANA outpost before

6. Kotizi

we were to wake up at 0500. Being the last man on guard, I was charged with waking up everyone so that we could prep and get ready for the mission. In order to do this, I approached the side of the outpost where all of the soldiers were sleeping in a neat little army line. I went down the line, tapping everyone on the foot with my boot so that they would wake up. Everyone but Sergeant Hunter; I skipped over him, hoping that he would be awakened by the sound of everyone else moving around. Sergeant Hunter was still not awake by the time I had got to the end of the file, so I doubled back to go wake him up. When I got to him, I ever so slowly reached for his boot, hoping that any second he would wake up. When I was but an inch from his foot, he yelled, "You're not the boss of me!"

Everyone froze, watching and waiting to see what would happen. As I stood there, motionless hand still extended, everyone burst out laughing. Before we'd left the States, he'd been notorious for scuffing guys up, so I was still wary of his demeanor. Not that he had ever scuffed anyone up for anything as trivial as this, but I just didn't want to push my luck.

Once everyone was up, it took us only a few minutes to eat, pack up and to be ready to step off at sunrise. Just as everyone had finished the life-or-death struggle of putting those ridiculously heavy rucksacks on, we got the order to stand down. I looked at Sergeant Hunter, who had just given the order, then at the chest buckle on my rucksack. I angrily unclipped it and let my ruck fall off my back to the ground with a dull thud. Everyone was confused for a minute or two, but we all came to realize that one of the units somewhere in the operation had failed to get ready in time for the sunrise step off. This meant that we would have to wait until they were ready. I found out later that it was the battalion commander who had failed to make the start time. This, of course, came as no surprise to me. The one motherfucker who was afforded the opportunity to ride around in an air-conditioned truck couldn't bother to show up on time.

I was so furious I picked up my rucksack just so I could throw it down again. Once it crashed back on the ground, I kicked it as hard as I could for good measure. Just to be a team player, Lemmon ran up beside me and gingerly kicked at my rucksack as well. He stomped around and pretended to be mad, even though he wasn't sure what I was being all grumpy about.

This type of problem would go on to haunt us throughout the deployment. Those who didn't have to do the actual physical tasks of the mission rarely fully grasped the consequences of actions of this type. Some may argue that these higher-ranking leaders were at one point in time in my shoes, that they were the lower-ranking officers leading patrols like mine, but this is oftentimes not the case. Many times, officers in command on deployments have never run the types of missions they are commanding, and many of them are on their first deployment. I have literally met generals who have never deployed before. One might think that this would be impossible given the amount of time the Army has been in Afghanistan and Iraq. Unfortunately, it is absolutely possible and happens more than it should. Nevertheless, he was the boss, and we waited for him to be ready before we stepped off.

    Four hours later, the commander finally graced us with his presence and gave us the green light to move out. We then all struggled to put those ridiculous rucksacks back on, filed up by the exit, and got ready to do just that. Some fifteen meters from the ANA outpost, we had to cross a small irrigation ditch that was about ten meters across and no more than knee deep in the middle. This is normally not a difficult task, but with more than 120 pounds of equipment on our backs, this turned into quite a spectacle. Blackman was mine sweeping, and thus he was the first to cross. Blackman was of average height and was built like he used to play football. He too was a Special Forces dropout and was perhaps the only person in the platoon who hated the Army more than Sanders. He was a very good soldier, and as a result, he got away with not doing things the Army way more than anyone should have. He had no qualms about taking advantage of the Army system and couldn't have cared less for things like badges and medals, or so he said. Blackman made the crossing look easy, but those after him were not so lucky.

    Everyone was slipping in the mud and falling face-first or flat on their backs. I heard a huge splash at one point during the crossing and turned to see nothing but a hand extended from the water holding an M4 straight up in the air. When it came to Sergeant Hunter's turn to cross, he was noticeably angry at the ANA, who had been laughing hysterically at the guys who slipped and fell in the ditch. Right before he crossed, he looked back at me, scowling as hard as he could, as if to make sure someone knew how pissed-off he was. He proceeded cautiously, but I could tell he was on unsteady ground. Just as he made it to the deepest part of the irrigation ditch, both his feet came out from under him, and he fell face-first into the water. After splashing around violently, he exploded from beneath the surface of the water. Trying desperately to regain his balance, he stumbled and slipped a few times before obtaining a sure footing. I could tell from the scowl on his face he was somehow even angrier than before he fell. He was staring a hole through the ANA dudes who were now losing their minds laughing at him. They had lost what little military bearing they

Blackman resting in a fighting position in the graveyard (Dick Mountain) (courtesy Brandon Young).

had, as some of them were doubled over laughing while others pointed and cheered.

Turning to look at the spectacle that was the ANA, I saw one of their soldiers throw his head back and laugh wildly. As he did, his finger compressed the trigger on his M249, and he accidentally let off a burst of fully automatic fire! I watched as the rounds traced a line in the water straight toward Sergeant Hunter! They zipped past his right knee, narrowly missing him and several soldiers behind him! This stopped all the laughter as everyone stood motionless. No one wanted to make the first move after that colossal blunder.

The silence was broken as Sergeant Hunter swung his rifle toward the ANA soldier who had fired the burst. Drawing down on the man, Sergeant Hunter centered the chevron in his ACOG on the ANA soldier's chest. As he flipped his selector switch to fire, the PL came running over in a desperate attempt to stop him before it was too late! He appeared to be running in slow motion as I stood there holding my breath.

Just as I thought Sergeant Hunter was actually going to shoot, the ANA first sergeant came from the rear of the file at a full sprint. With a skip and a jump, he slapped the ANA M249 gunner across the face. He hit the man so hard, his helmet flew off and landed next to my foot some three meters away. Satisfied with his leadership abilities, the ANA first sergeant nodded his head, put his hands on his hips and did an about face before moving back to his position in the formation without saying a word. While this was going on, the PL had somehow managed to calm Sergeant Hunter down enough for us to move on.

Most of the U.S. soldiers fell in the damn ditch as they attempted to cross, but now everyone was just laughing under their breath, trying not to draw attention to themselves. I, however, did manage to cross the ditch without falling in, and was quite proud of myself. But pride comes before the fall.

Due to the need for the Mine Hounds to sweep the way, we moved on at an incredibly slow pace. It was a necessary evil, but it was causing everyone to fatigue at an alarming rate. These rucksacks weighed more than the ones we had to carry earlier in the deployment, and they were crushing us. After a few hours of humping those damn rucks, we finally caught a glimpse of our objective. It was a large compound just a few hundred meters ahead of us. All that was left to do now was cross a small open field and an irrigation ditch, and then we would be home free.

By this time in the day, we had switched Blackman out for Lemmon as the minesweeper. Even from my position in the back of the file, I could tell that Lemmon was clearly exhausted. The fields that we had been trudging our way through were filled with thick mud, making our already laborious task even more difficult. I can remember looking toward the front of the file to see Lemmon using the Mine Hound more as a crutch than a minesweeper looking for IEDs. He would take one step forward, place the Mine Hound on the ground, place all his weight on it, then take the next step forward. He looked like an eighty-year-old man with a walker, just puttering along with nowhere to be.

Lemmon was, of course, the first to reach the irrigation ditch, which was only 150 meters from the compound. This ditch was about four feet deep, three feet across, and about half full of water. It was just wide enough and deep enough that one had to put considerable effort into jumping it or climbing down and then up again to cross it. Lemmon decided that he would jump it. He vaguely waved the Mine Hound over the ground on the other side and gave Sergeant Young a lazy thumbs-up. He then backed off a few feet to make the jump. As he made his strides toward the ditch, the amount of effort he was using was clearly not transferring to output. I could tell it took an incredible amount of effort for him to throw himself across the ditch. As he landed on the other side, he collapsed where he landed, and he became our first heat-related casualty of the day. He had used his last bit of energy to make the jump, and he was out cold where he landed.

With Lemmon no longer able to move on, we decided to leave a team with him, move on to the compound, drop our equipment, and then come back. At that time, we would help him into the compound. Before we could put this plan into action, the rest of us still had to cross the irrigation ditch. As I waited my turn to cross the ditch, I watched as guys were getting ridiculous head starts before attempting the jump. Despite their efforts, most men came up short and fell into the ditch. This meant that those on the other side had the exhausting task of pulling them out. This was no easy job, as getting pulled out was hilariously difficult, taking forever, and causing quite a scene.

Everyone had a hard time crossing, but Cristo had a particularly hard time. He was First Squad's Alpha Team M249 gunner and was around 5'6", 145 pounds. He was perhaps the fittest guy in the platoon and definitely the strongest for his body weight. He was Chilean by descent and never smiled. Not only did he not smile, he spoke in a monotone voice that made him sound like an emotionless serial killer. Despite his impressive level of fitness, he was still carrying almost his entire body weight on his shoulders. He too stepped off several feet for a head start, but once he reached the ditch and jumped, it looked as if he had intentionally run straight to the bottom of the drop-off. There was perhaps the tiniest little hop right at the end, but it was barely noticeable under all that weight. I can remember seeing his legs locked as they hit the bottom and shuddered under the weight of his rucksack. It was both hilarious and terribly painful to watch at the same time.

It took two men to pull him out, both of whom fell in more than once before they succeeded. After a few more people struggled across, it was my turn to leap the dreaded ditch. I really didn't want to make my life more difficult by falling in, but I was unsure of how to approach it. Once at the perfect distance, I ran hard and jumped harder. As I flung myself through the air, it was clear I was not going to make it. I landed on my stomach, half in the ditch and half out. I crawled and climbed my way out of the ditch, getting angrier and muddier with each movement. My only real concern at this point was keeping my rifle out of the mud. While I was clawing my way to my feet, Bertelli tried to reach down to give me a hand.

Out of principle for how much I disliked him, I refused his help like an angry toddler.

Finally, we were across the ditch and headed toward the compound. Once there, Sergeant Hunter told me to grab someone, go back, link up with Lemmon, and help get him to the compound. As one would expect, no one wanted to go with me. They all complained and bickered about how tired they were. Instead of helping, they offered up who they thought should go in their place. Sergeant Young, however, heard me and said he would be glad to help. As the two of us headed back to get Lemmon, I was fatigued, but I knew that the show must go on.

Once at Lemmon's location, we had a member of the fire team that stayed with him lead the way, while I threw Lemmon's rucksack over my shoulders. It took two tries and nearly all the force I had left to swing that thing up and over my head. As we moved back to the compound, the deep mud in the field started to take its toll on me. At one point, my rear foot got stuck in the mud as I tried to move forward. As my momentum forward waned, I started to ever so slowly fall in reverse, and there was nothing I could do to stop it. Just as I realized that there was no way to prevent the inevitable, Lemmon gently redirected my momentum forward, and off I went again. Reaching the halfway point in between our last location and the compound, Sergeant Young must have seen how tired I was, since he took the rucksack from me for the final leg of the trip.

Once back in the compound, Doc Gio attended to Lemmon with an IV while the rest of us settled into our security positions. Bertelli and I were positioned just outside the compound on a small kalat wall near a little path that led outside the village. After we had been in position just a few minutes, hundreds of Afghans started running out of the village down the path in front of me. There were old ladies carrying babies, children running wildly, and men on motorcycles flying between all the women and children.

Bertelli and I couldn't believe that not one of these assholes was helping these women with their kids. One man flew down the makeshift path with such reckless abandon that he knocked an elderly woman into that dreaded irrigation ditch. While we watched the stampede of people pass us by, Sergeant Hunter made sure that we were ready for what was coming next. He knew that as soon as all these people made it out of the area, it wouldn't be long before the shooting started.

This is the case because the villagers all knew what was going to happen before we did, and they were leaving with the knowledge of what was to come. At this point in the deployment, I had seen zero combat, and other than finding IEDs fairly often, it had been a pretty dull tour. So I thought this was a good sign and I was hoping that I would finally see some action. Maybe, just maybe, the vets would stop calling us all cherry fucks for a day or two.

Just as this thought left my mind, the M240 gunner on the roof behind me started taking fire. As I heard the bullets impact the wall, I can vividly remember thinking, "Here we go, finally!" I might have been ready, but I was in no position to return fire. Unfortunately for me, I was supposed to watch the west of the compound, and the element was taking fire from the east. The M240 gunner and others on the roof returned fire in what became a deafening exchange that everyone struggled to yell over. As this was going on, I just sat in position, scanned my sector, and pouted because I could not return fire. While I was feeling sorry for myself, I heard a huge commotion on the roof. I could hear Sergeant Young yelling something but couldn't make out what he was saying.

I looked over my shoulder just in time to see the ANA first sergeant firing an RPG over the top of the M240 gunner! As he fired, the back blast from the RPG hit Sergeant Young and another soldier, almost throwing them off the roof! The ANA first sergeant then stood there amidst the flying bullets with his hands on his hips, admiring his work. As he did, I watched the projectile he had fired fly way left of where any enemy could possibly be and detonate with a lackluster explosion.

While all of this was going on, on our side of the roof, Cristo was having his own friendly-fire problems on the other side of the compound. Cristo was nestled down between two ledges on the roof with his M249 on the one to his front and the other protecting his back. As Cristo was firing from his position, rounds started to come from directly behind him! After he'd dropped flat on the ground, he peeked up to see where the rounds were coming from. Turns out our M249-wielding ANA friend from earlier had started trying to fire over him with his own weapon, effectively pinning Cristo to the roof. He could not do anything but lie there and wait for the ANA soldier to empty his 200-round drum.

After the two ANA mishaps came to an end, the firefight waned and came to a halt. We had killed two of the Taliban who had attacked us. One had been killed by the gun team, the other by the sniper team, and the rest of them fled back into a dense tree line to the east. As everyone was high-fiving and congratulating each other for being a badass, I sat in my security position complaining to myself that I hadn't even fired one single round.

"Hey, Summerfield, that's a nice grenade launcher you got there. Ever use it?" I grumbled to myself. "You mean, did I fire any of these High Explosive Dual Purpose 40-millimeter grenades [HEDP]? Why, of course not, because I was pulling rear security like a loser!" I said, now almost at a yell.

While I complained, we prepared to move out and clear the next set of mud huts on our list. After completing our checks, we came to realize that we were almost out of water, and that the M240 gunner had gone through 800 of his 1,200-round combat load. Some of us were wondering why we were moving anywhere, since we were under the impression that this compound was the objective. In fact, it was the man in the air-conditioned truck who had decided that he wanted us to clear a few more buildings while we were in the area.

Before we moved out, I made it known that we were out of water, already had men with IVs in their arms, and could not move far without more guys going down. It was not so much that I was ignored, but that we had to keep moving to support Bravo Company. That being the case, First Squad moved out, leaving the support teams to pull overwatch and to keep an eye on the guys Doc was treating for heat injuries.

The next building was only 100 meters away, and we cleared it with no problems. We were told to set up security and wait for the trail element to move to our position. Just as I set Lemmon into the last security position on the north, we started to take fire from the east again. I ran back to the center of the compound, where I found Sergeant Hunter requesting mortar fire. He felt that we may actually be in trouble, because we had only six people to defend the compound. His request, of course, was denied, since higher command felt that there may still be some civilians in the area.

"The only people still in the area are currently shooting at us!" he said angrily into the radio.

"I'll get up on that shed and shoot some HEDP at these mofos, Sergeant," I said, hoping to shoot at least a round before it was too late.

"Well, get up there, motherfucker!" said Sergeant Hunter.

With that, I ran straight to a small outhouse on the east side of the compound where Bertelli was positioned. On my way to the shed, I ran into Douglas, who boosted me on top of the outhouse. As I was pulling Douglas up, Bertelli was letting off long bursts of 5.56 with his M249 behind me. Once Douglas was in position, I turned around just in time to see a few rounds hit the wall right in front of Bertelli. He got pretty excited by the fact that he was actually doing some Army shit as he looked at me to make sure I had seen what just happened.

As I nodded, I took a knee and opened the breech on my M203. I let the smoke grenade that was currently inside fall to the ground, grabbed an HEDP from my grenade belt, slid it into the tube, and slammed it shut. As I swung the M203 over the small wall in front of me, I thought, "Finally, this is what I have been waiting for." I pulled the trigger, and with that iconic "thud" the M203 makes, I sent the grenade into the tree line where the enemy was shooting from.

After it exploded, Douglas asked me to mark the same area with a smoke grenade so that he could talk some gunships onto the target. I then picked up the yellow smoke I had previously dropped and sent it to the edge of the tree line. As the "birds" approached, the Taliban tried to scramble for better cover, and while they did, I fired my M4 in their direction with reckless abandon. By the time the birds were on station, all those who'd opposed us had thrown down their weapons and fled to a nearby mosque. They knew we could not shoot at the mosque due to the fact that the U.S. Army had deemed this culturally insensitive. They were no match for the Apache gunship that had just arrived on station and they knew it. The birds spotted them by the mosque, but they had no weapons, and thus the birds could not fire on the enemy forces.

Once all the excitement had died down, the support element regrouped at the second building with my squad. After our checks, I sat down next to Bertelli to rest while the leaders decided our next move. We had no water and were low on ammo, but the PL wanted to push on and clear several more compounds. Since we had not eaten for almost ten hours, I was more concerned with getting a bite to eat while I had a minute to breathe. All the heat and excitement had diminished everyone's appetites, but I was going to try to eat something. While I waited for the next orders, I grabbed some cranberries from my rucksack. As I ripped the packet open with my teeth, I looked around at the other guys in the compound. The adrenaline was fading rapidly and being replaced by powerful fatigue. Just as I got my first handful of cranberries down, we were told to mount up. We still had several more compounds on our agenda that needed to be cleared. Having just gotten comfortable, I begrudgingly threw my kit back on. While I waited for the rest of the squad to get ready, I ate one more mouthful of cranberries and crammed the open packet in my pocket.

As we exited the compound. I could see that many of these guys were not going to make it far. The combination of the heat, excitement and no food was culminating in what would soon be heat injuries. "It's only a matter of time till I fall out of this shit," I thought as I counted the last member of First Squad out of the compound.

We made it to the next few buildings very quickly and cleared them with no resistance. Once there, Bertelli and I set up security on the corner of a compound to overwatch the rest of the squad's movements. As we were doing this, however, I was feeling worse and worse with each passing minute. Bertelli was looking paler by the second, so I was hoping we could wrap this shit up soon. Sitting there pulling security, Bertelli was certain he would die any second. This is, of course, exactly what I wanted to hear. I don't know if it was bad news because I was worried about him, or if I just didn't want to carry him back. I was on the brink of complete exhaustion, and I knew carrying him more than five feet would push me over the edge.

Just as I had decided that all was lost, the PL gave the order for us to move back to the compound. Relieved, I tapped Bertelli on the shoulder and we filed into the rear of the formation as they passed us by. "I only have to walk 200 meters, that's it," I thought. Every step I took became more difficult, and now I was worried about needing to be carried back myself. Just twenty short meters from the door, I started to vomit. With each step I took, I vomited again, leaving a trail of puke that ran straight to the compound door.

"Almost made it," Doc said with a smile as he watched me puke my way into the compound.

As I got in, I was ushered off to the side by Doc, who laid me down on my side under the little shade a small tree provided. Once there, I continued to vomit up what little water was left in my sensitive little tummy. After having rid my stomach of all its contents, I thought I may get a moment to rest. On the contrary, I started dry heaving, which at the time seemed more violent than the vomiting. While I continued to dry heave, Doc hooked me up with an IV and slid a poncho liner under my head. As Doc was hanging the IV bag in the little tree above me, I had a particularly violent fit of dry heaves. At the end of my convulsions, one single cranberry came out of my mouth and plopped out on the ground. It was actually quite funny to me and all of those who were sitting nearby.

In the end, we had six heat injuries including myself, which rendered us combat ineffective. But that is what happens when you carry too much gear and keep moving forward without water. This whole debacle left the PL pretty pissed off, because he had to call the man in the air-conditioned truck and tell him that we were done for the day. Not that I really cared who was mad at this point.

❈ ❈ ❈

6. Kotizi

The following morning, I was feeling much better, since Doc Gio had given me two IVs the night before. The day's objective was easy: all we had to do was move out a few hundred meters to link up with Bravo Company. Once there, we would help any way we could and wait for extraction. Upon arrival, Bravo told us to post up in one of the corners and asked us to rotate two guys into security positions on the south side of the compound.

The compound was quite large and comprised several rooms and two gardens within the compound walls. One of the gardens was filled with poppy plants, and the other was made up of a few small trees and cornstalks. We settled in on the south wall, taking as much shade as there was to take. We then started rotating two men at a time into our security position. The day went along quite lazily, since all we had to do was take turns pulling security and watch for the trucks to show up and take us back to Nalgham.

As noon approached, Lemmon, Cristo, and I grabbed some MREs and headed into a small room on the east of the compound. We were hoping to eat while at the same time escape the sun that was tormenting us. The room was the size of a large closet. It had a bunch of sticks piled up on one end, and several bags of rice lined up against one wall. As we entered, Lemmon plopped down on the sticks and somehow made lounging on them look comfortable. While Lemmon was melting into the stick pile, Cristo grabbed two bags of rice, threw one near me on the ground, and placed the other one down so he could sit on it.

As I sat down, I opened up my MRE and we all started chatting about the day before. Regardless of how lackluster it was, it had still been our first firefight, and I was glad that I would not have to leave this country and tell people I'd never fired a single round in combat. I can remember letting that first 40mm go and thinking how much of a relief it was that I did something, even though it was so minute and insignificant. As I was thinking about my good fortune and the relief it had brought me, Cristo and Lemmon busted open their MREs and we all started to eat.

"How the fuck are you lounging on sticks, Lemmon? Aren't they like jabbing you in the back?" Cristo asked.

"You just don't know how to lounge, man," Lemmon replied, dragging his words.

"I guess not," Cristo replied, shaking his head.

"Hey, you want those Skittles?" Lemmon asked Cristo.

"I don't know," Cristo replied in his usual monotone serial killer voice.

"What do you mean you don't know?" Lemmon asked, puzzled.

"You know exactly what I mean, Lemmon," Cristo replied, even more monotone than before.

"What the fuck are you guys doing?" I asked as they stared at each other awkwardly.

A moment later they both burst out laughing and Cristo threw the Skittles in Lemmon's direction. As they landed, they bounced once and came to a halt just outside of Lemmon's reach. He tried to grab them from his reclined position but to no avail.

"Goddammit, Cristo! Hand those to me," Lemmon said with a laugh.

"If I get up and get 'em I am going to eat 'em. So, if you want 'em, you get them," Cristo said as he stared at the Skittles, licking his lips.

With the threat of losing the Skittles, Lemmon got up ever so slowly, ensuring he kept watch over Cristo out of the corner of his eye. As his slowly extended hand grabbed hold of the Skittles, he yanked them up from the floor and opened them in one fast motion. He then pulled up his pants and slowly began to sit back down on the pile of sticks. Just as his

Cristo, Lemmon and Summerfield eating while the evil chicken pokes its head up from behind the stick pile. You can just barely see him in the far-left corner (courtesy Brandon Young).

ass started to compress the pile again, a loud "CUUOOOOOO!" exploded from underneath him. The sound startled Lemmon to such an extent that he jumped nearly out the front door of the room, tucking his long dancer's legs up to his chin as he leaped. He landed and immediately whirled around to face the pile of sticks. All of us were now motionless and waiting for someone to make a move. While Cristo and I sat frozen in place, Lemmon moved cautiously toward the pile of sticks, carefully scanning it for the source of the sound. Once within reach of the pile, he grabbed one of the sticks, jabbed the pile and out of it came another "CUUcooo!"

"What the fuck?" Cristo said laughing.

Lemmon peeked around the back of the sticks and said, "Holy shit! It's a fucking chicken, man!"

"A chicken?" I asked as we all burst out laughing again.

"Why the fuck did it not move the first time you sat down?" Cristo asked, still laughing.

Lemmon then tried to shoo the chicken away to no avail. Every time Lemmon would get near the chicken it would peck at the stick and squawk angrily. "This is the meanest fucking chicken I have ever seen," Lemmon said, genuinely surprised.

"Let it alone. Just eat, man," I laughed.

With that, Lemmon moved to the other side of the room. We ate our MREs and left the chicken to roost.

– 7 –

Unexpected Company

Now that we were back from Kotizi, I had to return to the day-in and day-out grind of force protection, or force-pro as it was known. On this specific day I was tasked with manning the Entry Control Point with Sanders. As we took up our positions in the makeshift dugout we called a bunker, we stared out at the desolate wasteland known as Nalgham. There were a few trees, an improvised dusty road, and a mile beyond that, nothing but desert. The desert somehow worked to make the day seem even hotter than it actually was, which was a shame, because it was already 90 degrees that morning.

In preparation for six hours of extreme boredom and unrelenting heat, Sanders took his ACH off and set it on the ground. As he was getting comfortable, I wondered how many pushups I would have to do if someone saw him with his helmet off. Some days I would have rather fought it out in Kotizi than do those fucking guard shifts. They could be brutal!

As Sanders and I sat in our bunker, we noticed an ANA Ranger flying down the road in our direction. The truck was kicking up so much dust I couldn't tell if they were alone or with a convoy of other vehicles. The Ranger was moving with such reckless abandon that tower one called us to make sure that we saw it. To them it looked like a possible Vehicle Borne IED (VBIED). There had been reports of VBIEDs hitting control points throughout the deployment, so it was not out of the question. Watching the vehicle round a corner a few hundred meters from our location, I could see half a dozen armed men in the back, all of whom were hanging on for dear life. One of them came so close to falling out. Two others had to grab his rifle strap and pull him back into the bed of the truck. Noticing a truck full of armed men heading his way, Sanders lackadaisically slapped his brain bucket back on his head. He then picked up his M4 off the ground

7. Unexpected Company

next to him and snapped his chin strap. It did little to secure his helmet, however, as it loosely dangled well below his chin.

Since the truck was full of armed men, we decided that a VBIED attack wasn't likely. This did, however, mean that we may be getting ready to participate in a two-on-ten gunfight. Starting to take the situation somewhat seriously, Sanders press-checked his M4, ensuring that there was a round in the chamber.

As they approached our position, they could either go straight or make a hard 90-degree angle turn into our Out Post. They were just a few seconds out, so Sanders and I took up positions behind cover and waited for the day to get exciting. I can remember debating which would be better: for the truck to fly right on past, or for it to power slide into a two-way rifle range. As I was weighing never ending boredom against imminent death, the Ranger slammed on its brakes in a desperate attempt to make that left. This time one of the men actually did flip out of the pickup and into the ditch. He did a complete cartwheel, head over heels into the shrubbery that lined the roadside. Sanders burst out laughing from amazement as he watched the man do a double-gainer into the bushes.

The driver then slammed the vehicle in reverse, backed into the ditch, rammed it back in drive, and floored it in our direction. They didn't even seem to notice that they had left a potentially fatally wounded dude in the ditch as they headed our way. At this point it was clear that this was no attack. They appeared to be fleeing from some invisible evil force that only they could see. When they reached our newly installed gate, four of the men in the back jumped out and tried to open it without our authorization. Sanders and I were screaming in English while they screamed in Dari, neither of us conveying anything useful. Amidst all the confusion, I heard someone yelling my name over and again.

As I followed the voice, I saw Amardad, our trusty interpreter, in the back of the ANA vehicle. He was frantically waving for me to come over and help him. I looked at Sanders, shrugged, jump the gate and jogged over to see what he needed. As I got within a few feet of him, I could see that he had blood smears on his face and hands. Reaching out as far as he could, he screamed for me to throw him a tourniquet. Before I could see who was hurt, I grabbed one I had rubber-banded to my chest plate and forced it into his outstretched hand. As I did, I finished rounding the back of the truck, where I could see what all the commotion was about.

My eyes first locked onto the bloody boot prints that were covering the truck's tailgate. I then followed them up to a semi-conscious ANA soldier who was missing his right leg from the knee down. Coming to realize the serious nature of the situation, I screamed for Sanders to open the gate. He immediately grabbed the latch and flipped it to the open position. He didn't know what was going on, but he was relieved to be done fighting with the ANA. The gate had to be manually lifted and was usually a chore for one man. This time its weight was of no concern to anyone. The four ANA soldiers who were fighting with Sanders opened it with such zeal that they nearly uprooted it from its position.

As they did, I attempted to jump into the back of the truck to help Amardad with the injured man. Much to my dismay, the driver pulled off at the exact moment I hoisted myself and my kit up onto the open tailgate. The combination of blood and erratic driving caused both of my hands to slip out from under me. Falling towards the ground, I barely managed to tuck my chin in enough to keep from bouncing it off the bloody tailgate. Having nearly hit my chin on the gate when the driver pulled off, I angrily and deliberately walked to where the truck stopped just inside the ECP. While I casually strolled along, I called the sergeant of the guard and requested a medic be sent down immediately. A few short seconds later, Sergeant Hunter gave me an affirmative that one was en route.

Once back to the truck, I made my second attempt at the tailgate, only to have the rug pulled out from under me yet again! Now furious at the driver, I yelled for Sanders to make him hold still while I climbed in.

"Sanders, make this fuckin' driver stay put for one second!" I screamed, taking my rage out on him.

Finally, as Sanders held the vehicle in place, I climbed in the back of the truck and helped Amardad with the tourniquet. He was starting to tighten it down just above the knee, but I insisted that we place it as high as possible.

"High and tight, man!" I said as we worked together to move it up.

Once it was as far up as it would go, Amardad cranked it down by winding the plastic windlass. I then checked his work by attempting to slide two fingers under the main strap of the tourniquet. I'm no medic, but it looked good to me. Knowing that this guy needed a professional, I stood up to check for any sign of our desperately needed medic. While I was scouting the winding path that led from the ECP to the main outpost, I threw the radio to Sanders. I needed to get a Nine Line MedEvac started and did not want to be interrupted by the radio while I did it. Just as Sanders clipped the radio onto his plate carrier, he received an incredibly useful transmission from the Tactical Operations Command (TOC).

"ECP, this is the TOC. Be on the lookout, an injured ANA soldier will be heading your way for treatment," an unknown voice said over the radio.

7. Unexpected Company

"Yeah, Roger, thanks for the heads-up," Sanders said sarcastically.

"Well, they are tracking what's going on, at least," I thought as I worked on the Nine Line. Everyone in the platoon was issued a prewritten laminated Nine Line card. This allowed the soldier to fill in the blanks without fear of forgetting any important information. Using it had never crossed my mind, however, since Sergeant Hunter had drilled us so much on basic Soldier Tasks and Drills. I wrote it in full from memory, including brevity codes. While finishing up the final section of the Nine Line, I could hear Doc Gio yelling at Sanders. He wanted to know where the casualty was and needed Sanders to point him in the right direction.

As Doc Gio rounded the back of the truck, I jumped down and he took control of the situation. Without hesitation he vaulted into the back of the vehicle and told Amardad to have the driver pull the Ranger over to the dugout. Once there they would offload the patient into the only shady spot within a reasonable distance. As the truck pulled over, Sanders threw down a stretcher for the injured soldier. Doc Gio then directed as we all carefully moved the man out of the bed and into the shade. As I did my best to help move him, I got a much better look at the extent of his injuries. A great deal of his face had been damaged from the blast. This is actually pretty common, since the war-weary soldier often walks with his gaze fixed on the ground. He finds himself doing this in an attempt to spot any IEDs that the minesweeper may have missed. Unfortunately, anyone who finds an IED the wrong way receives a great deal of damage to his face and eyes.

As Doc Gio went to work, Sanders and I tried to secure the gate in an attempt to bring some order to the chaos at the ECP. While we were doing this, the company commander came down with some random stragglers to help Doc Gio. In reality they just wanted to see what was going on, but they said they were there to help. While Doc was treating the man who had stepped on the IED, a second casualty appeared out of nowhere. He just sat down next to the man on the stretcher as if it were the most normal thing in the world, acting as if all the cuts on his face and hands were of no real consequence.

"Where the fuck did this guy come from, Sanders? I thought that there was only one casualty," Doc Gio said with a hint of anger in his voice.

I was just as clueless as Doc. All I could do was look around on the ground, as if that were going to give me some idea as to where the man came from. While Doc and I were trying to figure out what was going on, Sanders started laughing uncontrollably.

"Shut the front door! It's the guy that did a double gainer out of the truck into the ditch like an hour ago!" Sanders said between chuckles.

I had completely forgotten about the guy they had thrown out of the truck as they tried to power slide their way into the ECP. Come to find out, when he cartwheeled out of the back of the truck, he was knocked unconscious and everyone just left him there. He woke up with no idea what was going on and just wandered into the ECP, finding his way to the medic like any injured soldier would. It was a miracle that he woke up; he might have died had he been left for his ANA comrades to go back and save.

Once Doc Gio got the first man packaged up and the second man assessed, the CO called in the Nine Line MedEvac I had written. It wasn't long before I could hear the distinct whirl of two UH-60 rotors off in the distance. Radio contact with one of the pilots prompted Sanders to launch a purple smoke out onto the helicopter landing zone (HLZ), which they used to guide themselves in for an easy landing. After a few small bounces, the bird's wheels came to a complete stop. With the roar of the rotors calling them in, four men rushed the stretcher out towards the Black Hawk. Hanging half out of the helicopter, a flight medic awaited them with an outstretched arm.

Looking on from the ECP, I watched as they made the short 100-meter jaunt towards the medically equipped Black Hawk. As the four men shuffled in unison, Doc Gio followed alongside of the stretcher. He was carrying a bag of IV fluid suspended over the casualty so as to keep the Hextend flowing in the right direction. Their handoff was fast, and Doc Gio ensured that the flight medic received all the information that he needed. Those in the bird worked to strap the injured man down while our men turned back to our location. As the five men headed our way, the Black Hawks took flight, one followed by the other in perfect concert. Their rotors blew the final puffs of purple smoke away in a cloud of moon dust, leaving us with nothing but fatigue and the midsummer day's sun.

– 8 –

Jelly Legs

A few short days after our adventure at the ECP, I found myself sitting on the rear ramp of a MaxxPro waiting for a counter–IED presence patrol to begin. As I sat there, I heard the radio behind me crackle with some interesting information.

"SOG, this is Tower One. SOG, this is Tower One, over."

"This is SOG. Go ahead, Tower One."

"We have two men planting an IED in the road 400 meters directly north of our position. We are going to engage the targets, over."

"Negative, Tower One. Hold tight on that. I am going to request mortar fire on their position, over," replied the SOG.

"Roger, SOG. Holding, over," said Tower One.

"Fuck yeah," I thought. "Make it rain on those fuckers. Maybe this will postpone this patrol, so I don't have to waste too much of my life endlessly driving around in the dark under nods [night vision]."

Just as everyone was getting their hopes up, the radio crackled again.

"Tower One, this is SOG. We are a no-go on mortar fire. We are going to send counter–IED out to check on the two men. Keep eyes on, over."

"Wait, we are going to drive out and check on the IED?" said Sergeant Hunter as he approached the back of the truck where I was seated.

"Say again last, SOG. I thought you said counter–IED was going to check it out," Tower One inquired.

"I am also confused," said Sergeant Hunter with a sarcastic tone.

"Roger, that was the order," the SOG replied.

"So, we are going to drive out to an IED in the road in the dark?" I asked Sergeant Hunter.

"Apparently," said Sergeant Hunter with a look of disbelief on his face.

Just as we were contemplating how stupid this idea was, the PSG jumped out of his truck.

"Mount up! We are headed to Route Uwala," he yelled in his usual raspy voice.

"Of course we are! With all the options at our disposal, this was the best course of action our chain of command could come up with," I thought.

We all mounted up and prepared to head that way. I was the gunner in the second truck, which was a MaxxPro, with the PL as the truck commander. We were right behind Sergeant Hunter and Blackman in the first truck, which was the mine roller. Behind my truck was an ANA HUMVEE, and pulling up the rear was the PSG with Sanders as gunner in another MaxxPro. As I strapped in, I leaned down from the turret to see what the PL was doing. I really wanted to know if Tower One still had eyes on the men in the road. This was, of course, a big negatron, as the PL explained to me that they had finished what they were doing and headed off to the east towards Kotizi.

"Great, well, let's not find this IED the wrong way," I thought, as we exited the ECP. Tower One had seen the two guys place the IED just 400 meters outside of the gate, so we had very little ground to cover before we made it to the general area.

As the last truck exited COP Nalgham, Sergeant Hunter adopted a slow pace so that he could look for signs of disturbed earth, wires, or any other indication of the IED's location. This slow pace was causing the ANA truck behind me to grow impatient, which was evident by the fact that the driver kept swerving in and out of formation. The driver looked almost desperate to get a look at what was going on toward the front of the file. As I scanned my sector to the east, I kept an eye toward the north as much as possible. I wanted to know what was going on myself. As we crept on slowly and methodically toward the suspected site, the ANA truck had finally had enough of waiting for us to get there and broke out of formation. The driver then floored it to the front of the file. I watched the ANA HUMVEE pass my MaxxPro, then cut off Sergeant Hunter's MATV to eventually take the lead. Just as the ANA truck took point in the formation, I watched as debris shot straight up into the air, followed by a large cloud of dust and smoke!

"We fuckin' found it!" I said as I watched smoke and debris rain down around us.

The formation stopped, and the radios started going haywire.

"Contact front! Contact front! ANA Vic thrown to the east of the road!" someone yelled over the radio.

8. Jelly Legs

"Uwalaaa!" the PSG yelled into the radio.

Immediately after we pulled into our security posture, the PL, Doc Gio, and Douglas all jumped out of their respective vehicles and ran straight for the smoking wreckage. No minesweeper, no nothing, just straight to the point. As they reached the vehicle, they found it to be completely destroyed. It looked like it had been turned inside out. The HUMVEE had contained two passengers, a driver and a gunner. The gunner had been thrown more than a hundred meters from the blast site and through multiple rows of razor wire fence. The driver had been ejected through the roof of the vehicle.

Douglas helped the gunner to his feet and to my truck. Amazingly, the gunner looked almost unscathed and was able to walk of his own accord with very little help from Douglas. As Douglas approached the truck, he waved for me to drop the ramp, and I yelled at the driver to do just that. While the ANA gunner climbed aboard, I could see only just a few scratches on his forehead. I couldn't believe that he was one of the men who had been in the HUMVEE. Douglas, however, assured me that he was indeed the gunner. As I stared at the man in disbelief, Douglas exited the back of the MaxxPro, laughing about how lucky the man had been. "Holy shit. Well, maybe these two guys are just crazy lucky," I thought as the ramp closed behind Douglas.

The second ANA soldier, it turned out, was not so lucky. When Doc and the PL got to him, he had four amputations and was barely conscious. Doc immediately strapped hasty tourniquets on all four of the man's limbs in an attempt to stop the bleeding. As he did, the PL simultaneously got the litter off one of the trucks and called in a medical evacuation chopper. The HLZ was to be at COP Nalgham, since it was the closest and most secure HLZ in the area. This was a perk of getting blown up in your front yard, I guess. The PL and Doc then loaded the wounded man onto the litter and carefully placed him in the back of the PSG's truck. Then we prepared to evacuate the casualties to Nalgham. It took us almost no time at all to gather the wounded up and start heading back. As we rolled through the ECP, the bird was already landing in one of the fastest turnarounds I have ever even heard of during my time in the Army.

Once we were back inside Nalgham, several soldiers ran out to the trucks to help unload the casualties. One of them was the legendary duck-billed battle puss, aka Swoyer. As the battle puss quacked his way into the back of the truck to help Doc, he was stepping all over the poor injured ANA bastard's legs, or what was left of them.

"Dammit, man. You're trampling all over my man Jelly Legs here. Watch what you're doing, mofo!" Doc yelled at him.

"Sorry, he is taking up all the space," Swoyer said as he tiptoed around the back of the truck.

"He literally takes up half the space of a normal fucking dude!" Doc rebutted.

With that, Swoyer did his best to keep his battle fins out of the way while he worked. They then unloaded the man and ran him to the helicopter. Within a few minutes, both men were on the MedEvac bird and headed to the nearest hospital. As the birds took off, so did we. Wasting no time whatsoever, we all mounted back up and headed straight back out to the IED site, so we could secure it in a ridiculous attempt at finding the two men who had planted the IED.

Once back on site, we took up our security positions in the trucks while the minesweepers dismounted and started clearing out nearby areas for dismounted troops. While we expanded our footprint, the PL called for Three Charlie to come in and support us, since we needed more men for a proper security perimeter. All the while, I was scanning the surrounding area, which contained a few mud huts and grape rows.

Southern Afghanistan is covered in grape rows. They are long open fields covered in small three- to four-foot-high mud walls that run the distance of the fields. These walls are around four feet apart and have grape vines draped over them. They make for great places for both us and the enemy to seek cover and concealment. Additionally, there is usually about a foot of water in the bottom of them, which makes them safer to walk in than on dry land. This is the case because IEDs don't generally fare too well underwater. The components tend to deteriorate and rarely detonate after having been submerged for even a short time.

Scanning the grape rows and mud huts proved to be less than productive. All I could see was a few villagers watching us from a distance. For all intents and purposes, it could have been any two of them who had planted the IED, but there was no telling at this point. Unless they grabbed some AKs and started rioting in the streets, I would never know. While I was complaining to myself about both the futile nature of this search and the ridiculous manner in which it had begun, Three Charlie called up over the radio. They had finished setting up security and wanted us to know that the perimeter was secure.

With the all-clear, we left our dismounts to help Three Charlie. Then we took the trucks and headed back to Nalgham. Once we parked, I took care of my weapon system, cleaned out the truck, and headed back to the row of tents. On the way, I decided that I'd better look at the guard roster posted on Tent One to see when my next guard shift was.

"Sweet! 0400! I have almost 30 minutes!" I said out loud.

"Hey, shut the fuck up out there, cherry fuck, we are trying to sleep," one of the NCOs yelled from inside the tent, no doubt comfortably lying in bed.

"Well, I'm fucking not," I mumbled to myself.

After that pleasant exchange, I headed to my tent to grab a half-dozen Rip It energy drinks and then went to the ECP early. "At least I can relieve someone a few minutes early," I thought. Once I arrived, I let Palmer go back to his tent and I sat down for what would be an uneventful shift of arguing with the ALP and opening the gate for patrols. The monotony of the shift only made it seem longer. I was not relieved until noon.

* * *

Once relieved of my post, I trudged back to the tents, hoping to go to sleep for a few hours before someone made me do something else. I was so tired I was just barely dragging myself toward the rows of tents. Unfortunately for me, sleep was not in the cards.

As I approached the tents, all I could see was chaos. Between the two rows of tents, everything we owned was all thrown about on the ground. I could see guys who were doing burpees in one area while others held their rifles out in front of them in squatted positions in another. Those who were not getting in a workout were frantically searching through their belongings on the ground. There were no fewer than forty ponchos laid out in the walkway with all types of gear placed on them every which way. Squad leaders were demanding that we find something, but I couldn't figure out what. The first person I recognized in the mass of people was Lemmon. He was ever so calmly sitting on his rucksack, just waiting out the storm of stupidity.

"What the fuck is going on?" I asked Lemmon.

"I don't know, man, it's a layout," he replied.

"For what?" I asked impatiently.

"Fuck, man. I don't know. Something stupid, no doubt," he said in a lackadaisical manner.

"Goddammit! Fuck!" I yelled, super angry and tired.

Just as I was throwing my fit, the PSG came raging over to me and stopped me dead in my tracks.

"Hey you! Sandyman!" he yelled at me.

"Roger, Sergeant," I said, glaring at him.

"You! Go find Summerfield right now!" he screamed in my face.

Without missing a beat, I just yelled, "Roger, Sergeant!" then moved out like I knew where this motherfucker was hiding.

Leaving the PSG, I rounded the corner and went into a bunker that was surrounded by ponchos. There I sat down, took my helmet off, and lazily let it fall to the ground. I had not taken my body armor or helmet off for over sixteen hours and was pretty tired of this shit. As I sat there fuming, I thought, "This motherfucker just called me the wrong name then sent me to go get myself. This would be awesome if this whole debacle was my fault and I was fucking all these guys by sitting in here." As I laughed about this to myself, I decided that I had better go see what's up.

I took my body armor off and set it outside of the bunker next to Deegan Cole. DC, as we called him, was as happy-go-lucky as they made them, and unlike me, he never let the day-to-day bullshit get him down. He cared little for how the Army ran things and tended to do things the DC way. He was around my height with blond hair, and despite his attitude, he was a good soldier and a reliable member of any fire team. As I made my way out of the bunker, he was organizing his gear and placing it on his poncho for inspection.

"What's the deal, bro?" I asked.

"Summerhoss! What are you doing in there, little buddy?" he said, laughing.

"Oh, just taking a break," I replied with a sigh.

"I hear ya," he said, still laughing.

"So, what's going on here?" I asked again.

"Oh, you know, the PSG thinks someone stole his steroid needles and we are tearing this motherfucker down looking for them," he replied as he placed a magazine pouch on the poncho.

"No way? He is juicing?" I asked.

"Fuck yeah, bro! Have you seen him in the gym? He's benching MATVs, bro. Besides, we keep finding needles in the Porta-Johns, so someone's juicing," he said with a smile.

Just as DC was explaining the situation, the PSG from One Charlie came out of his tent and yelled that he had found whatever our PSG was looking for.

With that, our PSG stopped yelling, then headed toward his tent, went inside and slammed the door behind him. After a few minutes of everyone outside holding their breath, the PSG opened the door just enough to stick his head out.

"Clean this shit up!" he yelled, and then slammed the door again.

"That's a wrap, people!" DC yelled as he started to walk back to his tent.

"Hey, man, is this not your stuff? You were organizing it," I asked him as he was leaving.

"No way, bro, that's not my stuff. I was just looking busy, bro," he laughed.

"So where is your stuff?" I asked, somewhat confused.

"In my tent, little buddy. I was not going to move it all out here just to move it back in again," he said with a smile.

Of course, DC wasn't about to move his shit out. If anyone was going to show blatant disregard for an order and get away with it, DC was that anyone. As I headed back to my tent, I realized why the PSG was looking for me earlier. He must have wanted me to get my stuff and lay it out with the rest of the platoon. Still laughing at DC, I opened the door on my tent. As I walked in, there sat Lemmon and Cristo in the middle of the floor. They had their backs to me, so at first I couldn't see what they were doing. As I got closer to them, I realized that they were playing with a bunch of kittens. Lemmon had one little ball of orange and white fur cradled in his arms while Cristo used a boot string to tease two others.

"What the fuck are you guys doing?" I asked.

"We found kittens," Cristo said in his usual serious voice.

"Can we keep 'em, Dad?" Lemmon asked, looking up at me with a smile.

"Holy shit, where did they come from?" I asked, laughing at the two eight-year-old versions of my former teammates.

"They were just inside the tent when we came back in," Cristo said.

"Can we keep 'em?" Lemmon said again, impatiently.

"They could be our platoon mascots and they will do wonders for the morale around here, Summerfield," Cristo said with a serious look on his face.

I didn't care if they kept them, but I knew that if the PSG found out he would lose his shit. Stepping over the men and their kittens, I headed to my bunk. I was certain there had to be some Army regulation against keeping animals, even though I didn't know what it was. They did indeed keep the kittens, and the critters did indeed brighten up the moods of more than a few of the guys. While Lemmon and Cristo continued to play with their new friends, I decided I needed a little rest. We had to go out on patrol at 1500 that afternoon, so it was now or never if I wanted some shut-eye. The commotion over the kittens and the sound of everyone moving their gear back in proved to be too much for me, though. As all I did was lie in my bunk and think about how cool it would be to sleep for an entire night without any interruptions.

– 9 –

Seek and Defecate

The majority of the platoon stayed sick for quite some time after the mission to Dick Mountain. We all just seemed to pass the illness back and forth, never able to completely get it out of the platoon. One May morning, amidst all the sickness, we were charged with going on a short patrol to a small village north of COP Nalgham. Once there, we would enter the details of the villagers who lived there into a biometric scanner called the SEEK. The SEEK is a handheld device that collects fingerprints, retinal scans, and a few other pieces of personal data. This info is then matched against several databases of evidence that is recovered from IEDs and other attacks in attempts at making arrests and obtaining convictions. It is perhaps important to realize that no one in Afghanistan has Social Security numbers, identification cards, or really even street addresses, so tracking people is quite difficult.

The mission was only to last a few hours and we were going to take about a squad and a half worth of men. This brought our total to around fifteen. Despite the simplicity of the operation, the men were pretty sick and not overly motivated to go on patrol. I remember walking up and down the line of paratroopers who were to go out, doing my checks and thinking just how ragged and weak some of them looked. As I was inspecting them for ammo, batteries, and the like, I came to the end of the file, where Sanders was lying in a puddle of his own vomit. I knelt down, took one look at him, and then passed word up to the PSG that it didn't look like he could go on patrol. Given the simplicity of the mission, I knew that we didn't really need him to get the job done. As the word reached the PSG, he came raging to the back of the file where Sanders was lying on the ground.

"We don't need him, Summertan? How do you know how much manpower we need? Are you in charge now?" he demanded.

9. Seek and Defecate

"Roger, Sergeant!" I yelled as I helped Sanders to his feet.

"He's coming. Everyone, get ready to move out!" yelled the PSG as he gave the hand signal to move out.

"Jesus fucking Christ, what a moron," I said as he stormed off.

"I'm good, Summerhoss. Besides, if I die on this farce, I won't have to lie awake at night listening to Townsend snore like a baby seal anymore," Sanders said as he wiped the vomit from his cheek.

As we started to leave the COP, Sanders was vomiting every few steps and was being pulled forward by other soldiers. Watching all this transpire, everyone in the file realized that there was no way that Sanders was going anywhere. Practically the whole squad called the formation to a halt in unison.

"We can't take this fucking guy on a six–K movement!" the PL said with just a hint of anger in his voice.

Just then the PSG came charging back to where Sanders was bent over dry-heaving.

"What do you got, weak genes, Sanchez?" the PSG yelled.

"Roger, Sergeant!" Sanders yelled, snapping to attention sarcastically.

"Go see Doc, Sanchez, and I better not find out you were fucking around on your computer when I get back, Sanchez! Roger!" said the PSG.

"Roger, Sergeant. Sanchez moving, Sergeant!" Sanders replied as he headed toward the medical tent inside the COP for some aid and rest.

Back in our Army file, we stepped off yet again and headed to the village. Once outside of the gate, I realized that I did not feel all that great either. I might have felt bad, but I was grateful I felt better than Sanders. Before we made it even a kilometer from the COP, my stomach was killing me and my need to shit was at a level of urgency that I hadn't known existed. As we pushed on, I was walking along like nothing was bothering me, but was using every bit of willpower I had to keep from shitting my pants. With every short halt we took, we had to take a knee, which would present me with a new opportunity to lose control over my bowels. I was sure each time I took a knee was going to be my undoing. Despite my struggle, I managed to keep it together for several kilometers. At each halt, I would carefully kneel and carefully stand again, dreading each movement.

After what seemed like an eternity, we finally came within sight of the village. "I might just make it after all," I thought, since the objective was within grasp. I knew if I made it to the village, I would have a moment to rest and sit still while I used the SEEK. With that thought in mind, I returned to my feet and looked toward the front of the file. As I scanned the formation in front of me, I realized there was an irrigation ditch in between me and the village. As I looked at the ditch, I knew that it was going to be a problem. It was literally the tiniest irrigation ditch in Kandahar Province. It was maybe ten inches wide and no more than six inches deep. Everyone was hopping over it with such grace and ease. Of course, under normal circumstances, I would not have given the ditch a second thought. This, however, was not normal circumstances. I had been holding it for so long and with such force that my entire core was starting to spasm.

As I approached the tiny obstacle, I stopped to size up what could be my undoing. While I was contemplating my plan of attack, Lemmon came up from behind me. He was confused as to why I was staring at this tiny ditch as if crossing it was an impossible feat. Little did he know it was just short of impossible for me. The longer I stood there, the farther everyone else got ahead of us. I may have stopped, but the platoon had not; they continued to push on, leaving Lemmon and I behind.

With Lemmon urging me on, I decided that as long as I didn't jump, I would be able to keep it together. So all I had to do was place my rear foot as close to the ditch as possible, then step across, no problem. With my plan solidly formulated, I placed my rear heel as close to the edge as I could. I then proceeded to step across as gingerly as possible. Just as all of my weight transferred to my rear foot, the edge of the ditch gave way, and my foot fell the disastrous six inches to the bottom of the irrigation ditch. As I fell, I knew my fate was sealed. The impact of my heel striking the bottom of the ditch reverberated to the exact location where it was most unwelcome, bringing my fears into reality.

"Great! Just great! I fucking shit my pants," I said, quietly defeated.

At this point, I just put my head down and marched on, since there was nothing that I could do until I got back to the COP. I walked the last hundred meters to the village with a noticeably awkward stride. Even though I was waddling along awkwardly, I felt a certain amount of relief. At least I was no longer fighting with all my physical and mental willpower to keep from shitting myself. With this new-found relief, I moved into the center of the village, where the locals were being gathered. As I set up my SEEK and prepared to enroll the first villager, Townsend came up behind me and put his hand on my shoulder.

"You ready to SEEK these smelly Afghans?" he asked with a laugh.

"Oh, you know it," I said, thinking how great I must smell at the moment.

There were about thirty Afghan men of fighting age corralled in the center of the village for Townsend and me to scan with our SEEKs. We divided them in half and started to scan them one at a time. While I was scanning, I figured at any moment someone would realize how terrible I smelled and point it out. Much to my surprise, the powerful smell of the Afghans drowned mine out with great efficacy. Townsend and I made small talk while we worked, and he said later that he had no idea that I had shit my pants. The fact that we had no running water at the COP and that none of us had had a proper shower for well over three months probably helped to cloak the smell as well.

As I continued to scan the villagers, Douglas took a knee beside me. Turning to see what he needed, I could tell from the look on his face that something was terribly wrong. His mouth was oddly contorted and it looked as if kneeling was rather painful. Come to find out I was not the only one with stomach issues that day. Apparently, he had been desperately trying not to shit his pants since we had left the COP. When he found out that I had at least thirty more minutes worth of scans, he looked utterly defeated. Determined to hold the line, he carefully got to his feet and went back to his work elsewhere. Understanding full well his troubles, I hurried along with the scans as fast as I could.

While we were scanning the Afghan men, I told Townsend to send the ones who were finished to a spot behind us, so we knew who had been scanned. I did this because the men who were finished had begun to mingle in with those who had not yet been entered into the SEEK. This, of course, would slow us down and potentially fuck Douglas, not to mention we did not need the same guy in the system nineteen times. As I was making this sensible decision, the PSG overheard me giving orders.

"What are you doing?" he growled.

"Just scanning, Sergeant!" I said, confused and annoyed.

"Oh? I thought you were in charge now," he said.

"Negative, Sergeant, just trying to help," I stated.

"Well, you can help by hurrying up! Roger!" he said in his raspy voice.

We finished all the scans in less than an hour total and then prepared to head back to the COP. By this time my stomach was starting to hurt quite a bit and I thought, "For Christ's sake, I don't really want to shit my pants twice in the same day." As we exited the village, I was pretty certain if I could make it across that treacherous irrigation ditch, I would make it back no more demoralized than I was in my current state. As it came closer, my stomach started to hurt even worse than before. Thus, I was faced with the sad reality that my efforts may be in vain. Since my pants had only just started to dry up, I was getting pretty angry about the whole situation. I really didn't want to walk four kilometers with shit-filled pants, especially since they had just started to feel semi-comfortable again. I glared at the ditch as it drew closer, watching as the other guys jumped right over it, not one of them shitting their pants. "Maybe, just maybe, I could pull this off," I thought.

Once my turn arrived, I approached cautiously and from the perfect angle. I decided to make a small jump this time and attempt to land on the other side with the tightest butthole in Kandahar Province. Once I mustered up the courage to make the jump, I took two steps and leaped for the other side. As I took flight, I clenched just as tight as I possibly could. Much to my dismay, however, the extra tension that I applied to my core caused me to shit my pants just as I reached the peak of my flight. I landed on the other side and just burst out laughing. I was cackling so loudly that the PL stopped what he was doing to see what I was going on about. Turning to face me, he slowly cocked his head to the side inquisitively, clearly waiting for an explanation. While he waited patiently, I decided that the number of times I shit in my pants per day was my own business. So, I threw my hands in the air as if to say I give up and I won't do it again. Deciding that I was just being a weirdo, he turned back around and pushed onward to the COP.

I moved on, shaking my head and laughing as I again felt the relief of sweet release. The few kilometers remaining were easy going, and we made it back to the COP safe and sound. Somehow, we managed to make it all the way there and back without Sanders, a feat even to this day I can barely comprehend.

Once inside the gate, we circled up for a quick debrief and then were released to go eat some MREs. As I walked along the motor pool toward the tents, I saw Douglas walking as fast as he could to the nearest Porta-John. As I watched him waddle along like the battle puss, I knew exactly what he was trying to prevent. There were only 30 meters left separating him from his objective. As he got closer and closer, the look on his face became more and more desperate. Just as he started to reach for the door handle of the Porta-John, he stopped and hung his head down. With his hand still extended, he shook his head slowly and made the same face I had made earlier. He looked just as defeated as I did when I tried to cross that impossible irrigation ditch for the first time. After a short moment of reflection, he dropped his hand, turned to his right and went around the Porta-John. He then waddled back to his tent in search of a clean pair of pants.

"Holy shit! He almost made it," I laughed.

– 10 –

Gundi Ghar

With a clean pair of pants, I attended the brief for our next big operation. It was mid–June now and we were to conduct a mission in the neighboring area of operations (AO), Gundi Ghar. This AO was under the control of our sister battalion 2–321, and it was considerably more active than ours. Unlike us, they were in firefights with the local Taliban quite regularly. They had lost almost an entire squad only a few weeks earlier, and we were going in to help them take back control of the area. To complicate matters, the IEDs in the area were constructed completely without metal components. These IEDs, therefore, would have to be found using the ground-penetrating radar on the Mine Hounds. This meant that the old metal detectors that we carried as backups if we were to need them would be of no use.

The mission was to be a joint operation with a platoon from both Delta Company and a platoon from 2–321. Our element was to clear out the enemy forces from the villages in the surrounding area and secure a location for a future ALP station. Once it was secure, Delta and 2–321 would link up with us at the police station. At this time, 2–321 would secure the police station, leaving us free to clear the villages to the east. While we cleared the villages on our agenda, Delta would clear the villages to the west. We would not spend much time working directly with either of the other two units, but we needed to know their part in the operation. Once we cleared all of our building sets, we would then rendezvous at an ANA checkpoint, where we would wait for transportation to come pick us up and take us home. The whole operation was expected to take three days, and we anticipated heavy resistance throughout the endeavor.

After the brief, everyone began preparing for the mission by cleaning weapons and prepping essential equipment. I had a sit down with Sergeant

Hunter and we discussed the ridiculous packing list that the PSG had handed out. There was no way that we could take all that shit again! Our rucksacks had practically rendered our entire squad combat ineffective in Kotizi. Sergeant Hunter and I worked together to modify the list to suit our actual needs. Knowing that the PSG may inspect our rucksacks, we ensured that we technically had everything. We didn't want to get in trouble for working smarter instead of harder. Chipping away at the list until it was of a manageable weight, we were able to bring it to around seventy pounds total, including body armor. Even after losing fifty pounds of gear, we were confident that we would have more than enough supplies to complete the mission. After all the preparations were made, we all lay down for a few hours, because we would be headed out first thing in the morning.

We woke up at 0500 and were told to have all of our equipment ready to go, out in the motor pool by the trucks no later than 0530. Even though we had hardly slept, everyone was amped up and ready to go. Having heard that it was the most dangerous AO in the region no doubt had something to do with this. As I approached the staging area, I sat my rucksack down next to Townsend's. He had packed the entire packing list and his ruck dwarfed mine. He looked at my ruck, then at his with a confused look on his face.

"Holy shit, that thing is tiny! What are you taking with you?" he asked.

"Enough to fight a fucking war!" I said, pleased with myself.

"You are going to regret not bringing everything, man," he said, shaking his head.

"I doubt it," I said confidently.

"What are you going to do if the PSG checks your shit, man?" Townsend asked.

"Oh, it's all here, tough troop. Don't you worry about me." I laughed.

"OK then, where is your sewing kit at?" he asked skeptically.

"Sewing kit! It's right here!" I said as I pulled a single needle wrapped in thread out of a pouch on my kit.

"Holy shit! That's awesome." Townsend laughed.

"Don't you worry about me, Big Town. Ole Hunter and I have found a loophole for everything on the list. We don't plan on killing ourselves by way of stupidity this weekend," I said while I tucked my "sewing kit" back in my pouch.

We got all the trucks prepped and all gear loaded more than an hour early. Still, the PSG came out yelling and screaming about uniform standards and holes in pants. By this point in the deployment, his incoherent yelling was ignored by the majority of the guys in the platoon. People generally only listened to him when he was yelling directly at them now. He rarely had anything useful to say. He just liked threatening to fire team leaders if he found their men with sloppy uniforms, which was the least of my concerns considering we were going into an AO where the previous unit had just lost almost an entire squad.

Finally loaded on the trucks, we headed for Gundi Ghar. Gundi Ghar was a massive mountain outpost supposedly built by Alexander the Great when he was in the region back in 330 BC. Many of the men had read about the battles that had taken place on and around this key piece of terrain and were excited to see it for themselves. Once we were finally there, the day was full of mission finalizations, back briefs, and equipment checks. I remember two things in particular about the day: wanting to hurry up and get started, and Sergeant Hunter's demeanor.

While the privates went to eat at 2–321's chow hall, Sergeant Hunter talked to me about the mission with a certain uneasiness in his voice. This was quite rare for him, as he was always very calm and collected. We had been warned many times in the past of perilous missions, but they had all ended with lackluster results. Perhaps this time they had managed to convince even him that it was going to be a dangerous operation. Sergeant Hunter made it clear to me that if one of us was going to die on this deployment, it would be in this AO. Under no circumstances did he want it to be because we had forgotten to do something. With this sentiment hanging over my head, I checked and double-checked all my guys' equipment. I ensured everyone had extra occlusive dressings, more than enough water, and rifles that were in good working order. It never mattered how many checks I did, I always felt like I had forgotten something. After I finally decided that we were as ready as we could be, I gave Sergeant Hunter the thumbs-up. He then closed up the first aid kit that he had been inspecting and we headed for the chow hall.

The next morning, I woke up on the rocks in the motor pull at 0300. I use the term rocks literally: 2–321 made us sleep on the gravel where they parked their vehicles. The entire platoon was up early and ready within fifteen minutes. Everyone had done so many checks and rechecks the day before, all we had to do was throw our rucks on and move out. Despite our level of preparation and overall professional demeanor, nothing was ever good enough for the PSG. The normal yelling and threats were aplenty as we made our way to the staging area at the foot of the mountain. In typical Army fashion, we were on one side of the mountain and needed to go to the other side, so we walked straight over the top of the goddamn thing! As we made the climb, I watched as the other guys were being crushed by the full packing list. It was a rough climb for me, and I had half the gear they did. Once we reached the top of the giant hill, we took one last five-minute break where I did my final checks, and we locked and loaded for the day to come.

Once up and moving, we started making our way down the other side of the mountain. Our first objective was the closest village in Nadey. The way down the mountain was almost as painful as the way up. At one point we stopped and took a knee for fifteen long minutes. Not knowing what was going on, I just sat there angrily waiting to get moving. I could not wait to get this mission started. Later I found out that the lead team had gone the wrong way and was doubling back. After an eternity on the mountain, we made it to the first compound in the village. At the mud hut, Bertelli and I were posted up on the south side of the wall, pulling security. Or at least were supposed to be; what we mostly did was take turns pissing on the corner of some guy's mud hut. We had been hydrating furiously for the last few days and needed to piss every five minutes. "I'm not having a heat stroke today," I thought, as I was taking my second turn pissing in the corner of the security position.

Since we were the lead element in the movement, we were on high alert and expecting contact any second. All we had heard from 2–321 was that this area was insane. They told us that we had better be on our toes because they would be gunning for us. Ever vigilant, we cleared compound after compound waiting for something to happen. By mid-morning, however, I had given up on the thought of any gunfights. We just continued to drag along, bored and annoyed without any excitement. Finally, we came to within sight of the location for our tentative police station. The only thing that stood in between us and the tentative police station was a large open field. It was a large danger area that we needed to cross, so Douglas called for some gunships to cover our movement through the open field. The Taliban are always less likely to get rowdy when we have air support in the area. While we were waiting for two Kiowas to come on station, Nolan, one of the guys in the gun team, started vomiting. As I called for a medic, I was not overly optimistic about our situation. We had barely gotten started and we already had our first heat cat of the day. While Nolan vomited uncontrollably next to me, Bertelli proceeded to ridicule him mercilessly. It was his way of comforting the down soldier as they waited for the medic.

We had two medics for this operation since it was such a bad area. We had a brand-new medic named Hudson who was to aide our old friend

10. Gundi Ghar

Doc Gio. The new medic Hudson came over to take a look at Nolan. Hudson seemed a little apprehensive about the whole mission since it was so hyped up. In addition, he had only been in country for two weeks. Hudson ran an IV and started asking Nolan what the last things he had drunk and eaten were when the PSG showed up to help.

"Nolan, you got weak genes!" the PSG grumbled.

"You are going to be fine in just a few minutes," Hudson interrupted.

"Are you taking your Doxy, Nolan?" the PSG yelled.

"Doxycycline is only for malaria, Sergeant. It does not prevent heat-related injuries, Sergeant," Hudson tried to explain to the PSG.

"Aren't you new, Doc? What do you know about Doxy?" the PSG yelled as the Kiowas came on station.

As Hudson looked at the PSG confused, he headed off to prepare his element to cross the open field toward the tentative police station.

"Don't worry about him, Doc. He thinks if you take your Doxy every day you can't get sick," Bertelli told Hudson as he got to his feet, ready to move.

With the helicopters hovering overhead, our element crossed the open field with no problems. We then set up an overwatch position to ensure that the second element could make a safe crossing behind us. Once the entire platoon was across the field, we set up security while the leaders decided if this location was going to be suitable or not. While we had a moment to breathe, I made Lemmon and Bertelli eat some Power Bars and drink water. I literally watched them finish everything, since I was not planning on having any heat cats in my team that day. As I was doing this, one single bullet came out of nowhere and hit the wall next to Murphy. Murphy was one of the few guys in the platoon who had yet to see any kind of combat and therefore had no Combat Infantry Badge (CIB). Murphy was the kind of guy who spent all his free time on Facebook telling his friends all his war stories. He had even bought one of those KIA bracelets for someone in the unit who he didn't even know, and had it shipped to Afghanistan so he could wear it on patrol. Thus, he needed that CIB bad, because going home without that badge pinned on his uniform would make all his fake stories a lot harder to believe.

I scanned the direction from which the round came while taking a bite out of my own Power Bar. I was hoping that something would finally happen but figured that I was not that lucky. While I was scanning my sector, the ALP who were with us ran to the north doing whatever it was that they were doing. I could hear them fire several uncontrolled bursts, most likely at nothing. I couldn't see them but could picture them firing from the hip with their eyes closed like they always do. The whole ordeal lasted about two minutes. It left the platoon angry and unsatisfied, and Murphy with no CIB. He still worked hard to convince everyone it was worth a CIB.

"Hey, does that count for a CIB, sir?" Murphy yelled from his position.

"Shut up, you fucking pussy!" Bertelli yelled. I sure hated Bertelli, but he generally said what everyone was thinking

"Yeah, save it for Facebook!" Sergeant Young laughed.

After we had crushed Murphy's dreams of glory, the leadership decided that this building would not be a good site for the police station, so we moved on to the next potential compound. It was just a few hundred meters from our current location and would work well for our purposes. Once there, we dropped our rucksacks and left half the platoon behind to set in security and take care of the few men who needed IVs. While they set up a perimeter, my squad and EOD, in conjunction with Second Squad, moved out to clear the surrounding compounds. As we moved out, Sergeant Hunter asked what our water situation was. If we drank it sparingly, we had enough for an hour and a half, tops. My answer made him scowl even harder than normal, as he knew that 2–321 did not want to have to resupply us.

Sergeant Hunter passed my information up to the PSG, who didn't really seem to care; he just really seemed to like asking. As we exited the future police station, we split into two elements: the PL with us and the PSG with Second Squad. We all pushed on for the next few hours until we came to a large open area about 500 meters long. We again needed to get some air support to cross. It was more important this time since we had only about a dozen guys with us, four of whom were ALP. While we were sitting in the hundred-degree heat waiting for the birds to come on station, the temperature started to cause the Mine Hound to continuously throw errors and shut off. We had a backup metal-only detector, but considering that we were in a little-to-no-metal-signature–IED AO, it was of little use to us. To further complicate our predicament, the air support that we needed was promptly denied.

Despite these problems, the PL wanted to continue on to our final building sets, just across the open area. Sergeant Hunter, on the other hand, thought it was a terrible idea, mostly because the Mine Hound was not functioning. I didn't really care either way; I just wanted to get it done and call it a day before we were completely out of water. As Sergeant Hunter and the PL were discussing the idea, the PL decided to call the PSG

10. Gundi Ghar

to get a situation report on how they were doing with their building sets. The PSG said that their equipment was working fine and that they were capable of moving on. Later, I would find out from Sanders and Swoyer, who were minesweeping for the PSG, that this was absolutely not the case. They told me that they had been using their backup metal detector for at least 500 meters when the PL called in. After the leadership talked it over for a while, they decided to call it a day, and they thought it would be best if we headed back to the future police station.

Once back at the police station, we were completely out of water. The PL called up to higher for resupply, which was quickly denied. Some Kiowas that were flying by en route to another AO decided to try to help us out. They had one case of water in their bird, and they flew in super low and threw it out to us. Lemmon was on top of the roof pulling security with Denton when the bird flew by and dropped it. Lemmon said they watched in slow motion as the water fell from the bird. The two of them were licking their lips in anticipation as they watched the case plummet toward earth. When the water hit the ground, it exploded in all directions, shattering the two men's dreams of rehydration. This little debacle brought the water situation to a perfect end. We had no water, higher command said they wouldn't bring us any, and someone had just poured a bunch of water on the ground while we watched!

Since the water situation seemed to have no solution in sight, our interpreter Amardad decided that he would just go get water for us. He walked outside, stole a motorcycle from an abandoned house, and off he went to COP Nalgham. On the way, he ran off the road, hit an embankment, flew over the handlebars, and skidded across the ground. He then stood up, dusted himself off, and took a quick look around. Spying a van parked in front of a nearby mud hut, he decided he would steal it to continue on his journey. He then proceeded to drive the van off a bridge, wrecking it at the bottom of an irrigation ditch. At this time, he decided that he would just finish the trek on foot. As he was walking along the side of the road, some ANA soldiers picked him up and took him the rest of the way to COP Nalgham. Amardad then talked the ANA guys into filling the truck with cases of water and MREs. Then he convinced them to bring him and the supplies all the way back to our location. Amardad was welcomed back as a hero as the water was unloaded and divided up among the men. He acted as if he had done nothing, but his help no doubt saved the day. He could do all this, but the Army and all its power could not get water to us to save its soul.

Everyone started rehydrating as we settled into our security positions for the night. I took the first guard shift on the north wall of the compound. The police station was a larger four-walled compound with rooms built into the north side and a large garden that took up most of the courtyard. The garden was full of six-foot-high pot plants, which made some of the guys in the platoon pretty excited. As I sat down behind the sandbags in my security position, I started to realize just how tired I was. Tired or not, my squad had done quite well, and we had no heat-related injuries even though it had been much hotter than the mission in April. The guys who'd brought the full packing list had IVs in their arms or looked like they needed them. "I may be too stupid to plan a mission, but I can pack for camping," I thought.

After my guard shift, I lay down under a dirty blanket I had found in the compound. "If I can just get a solid two hours of sleep," I thought as I pulled the blanket up around my chin. Just as I laid my head down on my two-quart canteen, guys started jumping out of their sleeping bags and running around the compound. As I frantically searched for what was causing the commotion, I spotted a dark blur running toward Lemmon's

Thompson on Dick Mountain, maintaining an ever-imposing and aggressive security posture (courtesy Brandon Young).

poncho. As he dive-rolled out of the way, I realized that it was a fucking camel spider the size of a horse! Apparently, it had crawled onto a guy's lap, and when he threw it off, it started running from soldier to soldier, seeking refuge under ponchos and blankets. This was causing all the commotion, as one might imagine. As I was lying there making sense of the situation, I saw the spider turn and run straight for me. I was too tired to jump up and run away, so I just shut my eyes and hoped for the best. Right before the spider got to my face, the Radio Telephone Operator (RTO) Thompson threw his boot like a boomerang, killing the spider a foot from my head. It was such an amazing shot that we stayed awake talking about it for an hour.

Thompson was, like many of us, a Special Forces dropout and less than excited about his position in the regular Army. Being the RTO meant that he almost never slept, since keeping communications up and running was a difficult task. He did a great job, however, and was a good soldier who was always willing to help out even when it was inconvenient for him. After the excitement finally died down, a water resupply helicopter landed just twelve short hours after Amardad had helped us out. Despite its tardiness, we topped off our water. I went to sleep, knowing we had another long day ahead of us.

– 11 –

Gundi Ghar, Day Two

Morning, as usual, came much faster than I would have liked. Once out from under my borrowed dirty Afghan blanket, I woke up both Bertelli and Lemmon. I wanted them to pack up and be ready to go before all the yelling started. As usual, Bertelli got right up and started getting ready, while Lemmon looked at me like I had asked him to punch himself in the face. I then readied my gear and sat down to eat the remaining pieces of my favorite MRE, spaghetti and meat sauce.

By the time I had finished eating, the rest of the platoon was up and moving around. While guys were packing up, the PSG was going around handing out batteries for the THOR system. The THOR looks like a Ghostbusters backpack and emits a radio-jamming signal that is supposed to stop remote-detonated IEDs. When the PSG handed me the battery for my team's THOR, I looked at him and then at the battery, somewhat confused. I was confused for two reasons: one, what was the PSG doing handing out batteries? And two, he'd given me the wrong type of battery. The type of battery he'd handed me would fit in the THOR, but it would cause the THOR to zero out and crash, which would render it useless.

"Uh… Sergeant, this is the wrong type of battery," I said, confused.

"I know which battery goes in which piece of equipment, Roger," he replied dismissively.

"These fit in the THOR but it will zero them out, Sergeant," I replied, exhausted by his antics.

"Are you running this platoon again, Sammysauce?" he asked as he stormed off.

I went and grabbed the THOR from Lemmon, then took it straight to where the PSG was packing his gear. I slammed it down and started angrily undoing the battery compartment. Then I crammed the battery he had

11. Gundi Ghar, Day Two

given me in the back of the THOR. It immediately started emitting a high-pitch warning siren that was designed to alert the user that it would not work. Not only that, but it had to be taken to a service specialist to be reprogrammed and could not be fixed by a bunch of infantry idiots like us. I then looked the PSG straight in the face and handed the THOR back to Lemmon, who was to carry it for the day. While still maintaining eye contact with the PSG, I congratulated Lemmon as to the fact that he got to carry a twenty-five-pound useless piece of shit the rest of the day.

After my brief and futile moment of defiance, the platoon from 2–321 arrived and took over our security positions so that we could finish getting everything ready for the rest of the clearing operation. As we made our final preparations, the platoon from Delta Company showed up, which meant that we could move out and leave the police station in the hands of 2–321.

As I waited for the order to move out, I decided to go sit down by Townsend and chat him up a bit before we left. The moment before my butt touched the earth, rounds were fired at the northwest guard position of the police station. I turned toward the sound of the incoming fire just in time to watch a man from 2–321 fall backward from the position and land flat on his back. Certain that he was dead, I walked over to where my body armor was in order to suit up. It was almost impossible for rounds to hit those inside the compound; we were surrounded by ten-foot-high kalat walls, which is why I walked instead of ran. As I made the fifteen-foot stroll to my body armor, the sound of automatic gunfire intensified. A few paces from my kit, I passed by one of the guys from the gun team who had his face in the dirt, ass straight up in the air, hiding between Rodriguez's legs. I just shook my head, took a knee and threw my kit on.

As I strapped the chin strap on my helmet, I scanned the compound for my team members. Amidst the chaos of three platoons preparing to engage the enemy, it was hard to locate any one individual. Despite the confusion, I knew I needed to get my guys regrouped and on the roof. In the short time it took me to get kitted up, the exchange of fire came to a deafening roar. The first member of my squad that I located amongst the chaos was Sergeant Hunter. He was standing in the courtyard, gearing up with an annoyed look on his face per usual.

When I grabbed my rifle and stood up, I saw Lemmon already scaling the roof with Bertelli right behind him. I did a quick visual check of the two and realized that Lemmon was not wearing his gloves. One may think that this is a trivial matter, but not in this line of work. The PSG would lose his mind if he saw Lemmon doing any bare-handed gunfighting. After watching Bertelli struggle to climb the wall for a few seconds, I pushed him aside and climbed up impatiently in his stead. I wasn't going to let his pudgy ass stop me from sending a few rounds downrange. Once on top of the compound, I reached down and pulled him up to the roof, where I set him into the position that I felt was most advantageous.

While we were all struggling to get into position, the M240B was raging just a few feet from me, comprising one half of the two-way firing range. Right as I settled into position, all the firing stopped as abruptly as it had begun, before I had fired a single round.

While we waited and watched, hoping the bad guys would come back for round two, I told Lemmon to move to the north side of the roof. Sergeant Hunter thought we needed more security on that side of the compound. As he made his way over to where I had directed, the PSG caught a glimpse of those gloveless hands.

"Who does Lemmon belong to? Who does Lemmon belong to?" the PSG yelled like a maniac.

"He belongs to me, Sergeant!" I yelled, knowing full well what the problem was.

"Why doesn't he have his gloves on?" he demanded, showing me his gloved hands.

"I didn't have time for a parade inspection, moron. I'm trying to fight the Taliban here, man," I mumbled under my breath. I then turned toward the inside of the compound and demanded, "Someone give Lemmon his fucking gloves!"

As I waited for someone to throw up Lemmon's gloves, he smiled, pulled them out of his cargo pocket, and waved them sheepishly at me like a shy girl in an old spaghetti western. It was such a stupid situation I just laughed and got angry at the same time.

"Put your goddamn gloves on, Lemmon," I said with a sigh.

With the exchange concluded, we got off the roof and got ready for the actual mission. Once on the ground, I came to realize that the 2–321 guy I thought was dead was perfectly fine. He had just lost his balance when the rounds started coming his way and fallen backward off the sandbags he was on. He was already back in position ready for round two.

We were now ready to move out, with Odinson, Denton, and Townsend in the front of the platoon leading the way. Odinson had been a lumberjack in his former life and was built in accordance with that profession. He was a hard-ass to the point that it bordered on excessive, but he knew what he was doing and was a consummate professional. He was of Norwegian descent and could have been cast as an extra in a Viking movie quite easily. The Viking may have been in the front, but I, on the other hand, was way in the back. Being positioned second to last in the thirty-three-man file was quite discouraging for me, since it meant that there was almost no chance that I would be able to fire if we got into contact.

While our platoon was snaking its way through some grape rows some 200 meters from the police station, all my concerns were realized. As Townsend was sweeping the way, rounds started zipping toward him, Odinson, and Denton. The bullets were coming from a grape-drying hut a hundred meters to their east.

The three of them started returning fire as everyone else took cover and prepared for orders. Denton was firing his M249 on cyclic toward the grape-drying hut as Odinson swung his M203 over the kalat wall and took aim. When Odinson pulled the trigger, nothing happened! With no way to defend himself, he took cover behind the wall and tried to clear the malfunction. With Odinson out of the fight, Townsend stepped up and started to call out enemy locations for Denton to engage.

"Enemy contact 100 meters twelve o'clock!" Townsend yelled.

Denton then swung his M249 toward the target that Townsend had called out. Just as Denton caught a glimpse of the enemy Townsend had pointed out, he burst out laughing.

"Oh, Townsend, that's not a bad guy, that's a haystack." Denton laughed as more rounds whizzed over the two men's heads.

As Denton and Townsend continued to engage Taliban haystacks, Swoyer came running up to help Odinson with his weapon system. Odinson had been struggling with the safety that was jammed for some unknown reason. With just one look at the weapon, Swoyer clicked the safety to the side and it broke free. With a look of disbelief, Odinson swung the M203 back over the kalat wall. He then sent the HEDP inside toward the grape hut containing all the Taliban and their evil haystacks. With all four weapon systems up and running, the four men were able to rain down an impressive amount of fire on the enemy.

Despite the hilarious confusion, those in the front of the element were able to suppress the bad guys and force them to retreat, at least for the moment. As we picked up and continued forward, I complained about being stuck in the back of the element with nothing to do but watch everyone else be a badass. I decided that I might be of more use to the platoon as the designated water boy. I could just wait for all the gunfighters to get thirsty and then I would run up to the front and let them get a few sips out of my CamelBak.

While I was complaining, the leadership decided that we should start using a technique called bounding overwatch. This means that half the platoon would move forward while the other covers them. This is a much slower means of movement, but it provides much better security.

With my squad set into the overwatch position, Townsend and crew continued toward the first set of compounds on the agenda. They made it less than 200 meters before they came under fire from two enemy machine-gun teams equipped with PKMs. This time, they kicked the door in on the nearest compound so that they could fight from a more fortified position. Upon entering the compound, Park jumped up on the roof, adopted a power stance, and started firing the M240B machine gun from the hip. He did this for two reasons: one, so as to provide cover fire for those getting into position; and two, because he thought it would be awesome.

Once everyone else was in position, they attempted to establish fire superiority over the enemy machine-gun teams. Both elements were firing on cyclic, which meant that they were spraying bullets toward one another at upwards of 900 rounds a minute. While the gun teams unloaded on each other, the squad leaders screamed orders in an attempt to control the chaos. Amidst the confusion, Thompson called up to higher command that our unit was in contact while he moved into a position to return fire. Once off the radio, he jumped up on a ledge in front of a kalat wall where he could see the enemy positions. Just as he swung his rifle over the ledge, he started to vomit and fell backward off the ledge, landing on his back. Heat injuries started early that day and would only worsen as the day went on.

A hundred and fifty meters behind Townsend's element, Lemmon and I watched intently from our position next to an abandoned compound. We were hoping to catch some of the Taliban fighters out in the open as they fled. We were cautious, however, because we did not want to fire wildly and risk hitting any friendlies in the process. Lemmon was to my left lying prone, while I stood completely upright, scouring the enemy's position and looking for a clear shot. I glanced over at him to ask if he could see anything, just in time to see a few rounds strike the dirt a few feet from his head.

"You better get down, dude," Lemmon said in his normal easygoing tone.

"Oh, I'm good, man. It's just a few stray rounds," I said as I turned my attention back to the engagement in front of us.

"Dammit, man. At least take a knee," Sergeant Hunter said as he checked the security perimeter behind us.

11. Gundi Ghar, Day Two

I complied, not really thinking much about it. I just didn't want to miss a chance to shoot; that was my only real concern.

As Lemmon and I scanned the area in front of us, a MedEvac call came over Sergeant Hunter's radio behind us. This, of course, meant that someone in the other element had been injured in the exchange. We came to find out that the hero of yesterday, Amardad, had jumped up on top of one of the compound walls, fully exposing himself while he fired his AK47. While acting out this scene from an action movie, he took two rounds to the thigh. After being hit, he just calmly walked over to the PL and told him that he had been shot. The PL, of course, thought that he was just being silly, given his uncharacteristically calm demeanor. It wasn't until Amardad showed him the blood on his thigh that he started to take him seriously. After coming to realize the serious nature of the situation, the PL called for the medics to attend to Amardad. As Doc Gio dressed Kahn's wounds, Townsend and friends finished off the enemy for the time being.

We now needed to secure an HLZ for Amardad. So my element moved up to a compound that would provide cover for those who would move out to meet the bird when it came in. Our squad took over a standard little mud hut with four walls, a few rooms on each side, and a large open area in the middle. Upon entry, Sergeant Hunter had me secure the ground floor and the entrance of the compound with my guys. Then he took the roof with the other half of the squad to overwatch the HLZ.

Just as I got the guys into position, one of the headquarters dudes we had brought started snooping around the rooms on the east side of the compound. He was peeking into each room one at a time till he came to a small doorway in the corner of the courtyard. For some reason, the entrance to the room had been blocked with a few small branches. As he peered in, he noticed something moving around inside.

"Hey, guys, there is a cow in here!" he shouted.

"Well, leave it the fuck alone," I yelled over my shoulder while scanning the area outside of the compound entrance.

"He's a nice cow, bro. That's a good cow," he said as he reached his hand out to pet the cow.

Just as he touched it on the head, the "cow" became a bull and it exploded from the little room. The bull charged from its refuge, narrowly missing the turd from headquarters. It then proceeded to buck wildly around the open courtyard, charging and thrashing in every direction. Everyone in the courtyard immediately stopped what they were doing to avoid being trampled by the bull. We looked like a bunch of rodeo clowns as we jumped and dived out of the bull's path. At one point, the bull charged straight toward me by the entrance. With no other option, I was forced to step outside where rounds were zipping by in order to avoid being trampled.

As we came to the conclusion that we were going to have to shoot the bull, a tiny old Afghan lady no less than a thousand years old came out of one of the side rooms. The Afghan men oftentimes leave the women to fend for themselves when all the fighting starts, so this was not uncommon. What was uncommon was that she beat the bull in the face with a scarf till it ran back into its little room with its tail between its legs—which was much the way that we felt after seeing her handle business so easily. At the conclusion of the rodeo, Sergeant Hunter yelled down that the MedEvac bird was taking off and for us to regroup. We were going to link up with Townsend's element.

We left the mud hut and headed toward the next nearest compound to our east. As we approached, I could see Park and Rodriguez, who were pulling security in a small irrigation ditch. The ditch was just a few feet from the entrance of the compound where the rest of the platoon had regrouped. Having heard a war movie's worth of rounds expended, I came over to see if the two of them had gotten to kill any bad guys with their M240B. Rodriguez couldn't have cared less about fighting bad guys, however, because he had just seen a camel for the first time in his life. He was so excited he couldn't talk to me about anything else. Wanting to see what all the fuss was about, I turned toward the direction that Rodriguez was pointing. There it was, in all its splendor, a lone camel standing in the only shaded spot for miles. As I moved on toward the compound's entrance, Rodriguez was looking at the camel like an eight-year-old in a petting zoo, just as content as he could possibly be.

When I entered the small compound, most of the platoon was resting near the walls while Townsend and Harris were on the roof exchanging fire with some bad guys way off in the distance. Once in the center of the courtyard, Sergeant Hunter told me that we would be taking lead and heading out in fifteen minutes. This was the good news that I had been waiting for all day. Perhaps, just maybe, I could fire a few rounds at all the deadly haystacks that had been attacking my teammates all morning long.

While waiting to move out, I noticed that near me in the center of the courtyard there was an ancient Afghan man. He was squatting like a catcher and using a stick to prod at a defenseless beetle that had been trapped on its back. As I made eye contact with him, he showed me his teeth, all of which looked like they had been filed to points.

"Alrighty then," I said as I pulled a bag of Skittles out of my lowest

11. Gundi Ghar, Day Two

pants pocket. Several of us carried Skittles in our calf pocket. That way, when we stepped on an IED, everyone else could taste the fuckin' rainbow. This, of course, was Sanders's idea originally.

I opened the bag and started to walk toward Lemmon and Doc Gio, who had taken a seat under a small tree in the compound. It was so dilapidated it provided no shade, but was at least something to lean up against. As I got closer to where Lemmon and Doc were seated, both of their jaws dropped open. As I looked at the two men, confused, Lemmon slowly raised his hand and pointed to something behind me. I then slowly turned around to see the ancient squatting man hopping after me, making grabbing motions in the air. He looked like a cross between a spider and a troll on the prowl.

I nodded to the spider troll and whipped my head around toward Lemmon. Then, in a very matter-of-fact tone, I stated, "Clearly a case of squat-o-manthomia. It's a serious problem in these parts." We all laughed, and the man just squatted on past me, looking for other people to spider troll.

After I explained to Lemmon the medical conditions that impacted the region, our squad prepared to move out. We filed up on the door where Sergeant Hunter explained that we were to move into the irrigation ditch in front of the compound. Once inside, we would use it as cover and concealment for roughly 200 meters. We would then exit the ditch into a nearby set of grape rows and set in an overwatch position. Then Townsend's element would leapfrog us to the next compound. At that point, we would all regroup and plan our next move.

The irrigation ditch was about five feet deep and four feet wide, with just a few inches of water in the bottom of it. As we made our way through, Sergeant Hunter realized that we needed to cross a small danger area to get into our overwatch position. From the looks of it, we would be completely exposed for about eight meters when we exited the irrigation ditch and crossed into the grape rows. He made sure that every man in the squad knew to cross the danger area one at a time. We didn't want to give the enemy the opportunity to catch more than one of us out in the open at once. Just to be sure that everyone was on the same page, each man passed the order back right before he crossed the open area. As I waited for my turn to make the crossing, I scanned my sector and ensured that my team had good spacing.

Once those in front of me had crossed, I climbed out of the ditch and quickly vaulted the four-foot kalat wall. Now that I was across, I took up a security position and motioned for Bertelli to follow suit. He struggled out of the ditch and made his way to the kalat wall. As he jumped, he got high centered on the barrier. Half his body was on one side while the other half dangled on the other. He had gotten his pudgy belly stuck in a low spot on the wall where he had attempted to cross. As he struggled, his rucksack fell over his head like a jersey in a hockey fight. He was completely stuck, ass-exposed to the enemy, about which Sergeant Hunter had warned us. This enraged me to no end for some ridiculous reason. I grabbed his rucksack, pulled him over, and watched him crash to the ground like a sack of potatoes. As he lay in a broken pile of Army equipment and fatigue, I cursed at him in an attempt to add insult to injury. Bertelli was, of course, unfazed by my incoherent ramblings. He just collected himself, stood up and got into position on the wall where he could pull security. Once there he gave me a big smile and thumbs-up as if to show me just how unfazed he was.

As we sat in our security positions, we waited a really long time for Townsend's element to leapfrog us. It should not have taken them but a few minutes to reach our location, and I was starting to grow impatient. When they finally started to trickle in, I realized what was taking so long. Many of the men in the other element were near heat exhaustion and they were almost out of water. I vividly remember seeing Sanders struggle to climb the kalat wall next to me with the entire packing list on his back. I had no idea how he could even move with all that weight on his shoulders. When Bertelli and I pulled him over the wall, he fell to the ground at our feet and was unable to stand of his own accord. We helped him up and then some guys took him to a shady spot where Doc Gio took a look at him.

Shortly after Sanders crossed the wall, I watched in disbelief as guys started to come across the barrier carrying two rucksacks at a time. Some of the other guys who had packed the whole list were now too weak to carry their own equipment. Once I saw this, I knew we were in trouble. No one can carry two rucksacks for too long without going down themselves. The more guys who went down meant that more guys would go down, as fewer and fewer people would have to carry more and more equipment.

Once about half of the platoon was in the grape row, Townsend, DC, and Odinson all tried to climb out of the irrigation ditch at the same time.

Just as I yelled, "One man at a time!" a PKM opened fire on our position.

As the rounds crashed into the kalat wall around the three men, they froze. They were momentarily unsure of whether they should climb the wall or hit the deck.

11. Gundi Ghar, Day Two

As I raised my rifle to return fire, Odinson yelled, "In the ditch!"—which prompted the three men, almost in unison, to leap back into the ditch they had just exited. While returning fire, I noticed that someone had marked the enemy position with a yellow smoke grenade.

As I redirected my fire toward the smoke, Sergeant Hunter yelled, "Summerfield, HEDP max range!" The sound of gunfire from both sides was deafening, and it was a miracle that I heard him at all.

I stood up from where I was kneeling behind the wall and fired a grenade into the doorway of the building marked by the yellow smoke. As it exploded, earth was flung some twenty feet in the air, obscuring the target momentarily.

As bullets whizzed and cracked over my head, I slid open the tube of my M203 and slammed another grenade into the breech. I then swung it back on target and fired while yelling, "Fuck yeah!" I was just thankful I finally got to shoot. Later Townsend would tell me that he heard someone yelling "fuck yeah" and wondered who was having such a good time.

I ran through all twelve HEDP I had on my kit and yelled, "HEDP! I need HEDP!" I then started to fire rounds from my M4 'til it ran dry. At that time, I took a knee behind the wall to reload. Just as I grabbed a fresh magazine from my kit, bullets whizzed over my position and one smashed into the wall by my head. The impact of the round was so close it caused me to lose my hearing for a short while, leaving me with that ringing sound we always hear in the movies after an explosion. This might have been cool except for the fact that the problem still persists to this day.

As I tried to shake off the ringing in my ears, I slammed the fresh magazine in my hand into my rifle. "HEDP!" I yelled again as I hit the bolt release on my M4.

This time, I looked down the line of men firing to see if anyone had heard me. Instead, all I saw was Blackman sitting on the ground reclining against his rucksack. He had his hands behind his head and was taking a break! As I was trying to comprehend what Blackman was doing, Palmer handed me a fresh belt of HEDP. I slung the belt over my head and then nodded to Palmer as thanks. Now reloaded, I fired a few bursts from my M4 before I opened the breech on the M203. As I again started letting the M203 rounds go like they were on sale, I saw Odinson doing the same. Forty-millimeter grenades travel slow enough that you can watch them fly to their target. I watched as my rounds and Odinson's rounds synced up in the air and hit their mark simultaneously in one massive explosion.

While I was marveling at my and Odinson's duo of destruction, Douglas yelled that he needed another smoke on target for the gunships that were coming on station.

"I got it!" I yelled.

I fired the HEDP in the tube, then opened the breech on the M203 and slid a yellow smoke into the chamber. By this time, the fire had slowed to a more constant pace, and Townsend was facing my direction from the ditch.

"Take your time," he said in a calm voice.

After a careful aim, I let the smoke fly right in through the front door of the building. Douglas then directed the gunships to their target. They arrived just in time for the fight to be over, since all the bad guys were either dead or gone. After a few circles overhead, they headed off to refuel, leaving us to our own devices. With the coast clear, the rest of the men got over the wall, where we regrouped and prepared to clear the rest of the surrounding area.

Now that all the excitement had subsided, we checked ammo and water, and looked for injuries. All was good except for the several heat injuries that we had incurred prior to the firefight. There were at least seven men who were too weak to carry their own equipment. To make matters worse, Sanders, who had been incredibly weak earlier, was now completely unconscious. These new developments prompted us to prepare a litter for Sanders, who would have to be carried. We then divided the seven men's equipment up among the platoon so as not to burden one man with too much equipment. While we divided up the gear, the PSG sent ten men on ahead to secure the next compound on our list.

Once we got word over the radio that the compound was secure, we got everyone to their feet and prepared to move out. Even after the equipment had been divided up, everyone was still carrying so much gear I thought we would never make the short 400-meter movement. I had all my gear, my rucksack plus an additional man's assault pack, my rifle, a M249 machine gun, Sanders's body armor, and the front right side of the litter that Sanders was on. I tried to put Sanders's armor back on him prior to movement but the PSG told me otherwise.

"Stop being a pussy and just carry it, Sandyville. Sanchez don't need that shit!" the PSG yelled.

So off we went. We carried the litter over grape rows, over walls, and through the mud in the bottom of the rows. While I carried the litter, my vision was constantly fading in and out. I would go from clearly seeing what was in front of me to just two little pinholes of vision from which to see the world. It was 108 degrees that day and way too hot for this shit. It took every ounce of strength I had to keep moving forward with that litter.

As we got within 200 meters of the compound, the Taliban in the area started taking pot shots at those of us carrying the litter. We were an easy target, all grouped together around Sanders. All we could do was just plug along as the other guys returned fire to cover our movement. Even though I could hear the rounds zipping overhead, I was more concerned about passing out than being hit by a stray bullet. I could feel consciousness slowly escaping me with each step I took, and I knew it was only a matter of time.

We eventually made it to the compound, tired but unscathed. Once inside, we placed Sanders in a room indicated by Doc Gio. Seeing that Sanders was taken care of, we started to further secure the compound as directed by the squad leaders. As the security perimeter took shape, the PL sent Second Squad out front of the compound to secure a large open field. Sanders was still unconscious, and Doc feared he may actually die in the 108-degree heat. Thus, we needed to secure an HLZ so that a MedEvac helicopter could land and take him to a hospital for proper treatment.

This particular compound was larger than most, and had two courtyards inside with rooms lining three of the four walls. There was a four-foot-deep irrigation ditch that ran in front of it, effectively creating a moat. Beyond the ditch, there was a large open field that was lined with trees and shrubs some 300 meters from the structure. The surrounding area was littered with smaller compounds and irrigation ditches, as well as a few abandoned motorcycles and goats that the locals had left in their haste to escape the war zone.

Inside the compound, the minesweepers cleared the area meticulously for the machine-gun teams and designated marksman. The heat was proving too much for the Mine Hounds, though, and they constantly faded in and out. This, of course, meant the PSG was starting to grow impatient because of the equipment's shortcomings. As he grew more frustrated, the PSG started to look for someone to take his anger out on. Even though Townsend was doing everything within his power to keep the Mine Hound running, the PSG began to focus in on him. As a testament to his efforts, Townsend had even used the last of his precious water to keep the Mine Hound cool. He had wet a T-shirt and wrapped it around the Mine Hound, hoping this would keep it cool enough to operate. Despite his efforts, he still had to turn the Mine Hound off every so often to let it cool down. While Townsend was standing at the limits of his mine-swept lane, resetting the Mine Hound, the PSG started freaking out that he was standing still and not sweeping. Out of the corner of his eye, Townsend could see that the PSG was about to lose his shit and start screaming at him. So Townsend started to freak out himself, swearing and shaking the Mine Hound violently.

"Work, you fucking piece of shit!" Townsend screamed at the Mine Hound.

He then rape-choked and punched the Mine Hound repeatedly. His ridiculous antics seemed to satisfy the PSG's lust for rage, as he just nodded his head in approval and headed off to find someone else to yell at. The PSG could not operate like a normal person and Townsend knew this. Perhaps he had been in the Army too long; perhaps it was the steroids. Who knows? But Townsend had figured him out. Once it was reset, Townsend used the Mine Hound to clear the rest of the compound. After he declared all areas safe, we were allowed to move around the mud hut freely.

The main entrance of the compound was locked, which meant that when Second Squad returned from clearing the landing zone, someone had to let them in. As they approached, Odinson yelled down from the roof that they were on their way back. I was taking my helmet off when he got my attention. So I set my helmet on my rucksack then went and unlocked the door to let them in. Just as I opened the door, the tree line adjacent to the compound erupted in gunfire aimed at Second Squad. They all ran straight into the compound, almost trampling me in the process.

I wanted to get in the fight, so I ran, grabbed my helmet and strapped it on. Then, as fast as I could, I sprinted back toward the door. As I approached, I could hear rounds hitting the wall around the door and zipping overhead. Just as I reached the exit, there, blocking my way, was Nolan. He was half in and half out of the compound, deciding if he wanted to make the short run through the hail of bullets to the irrigation ditch out front. Just the sight of him there pissed me off. He was stutter-stepping in the entryway like a little kid too scared to jump off the high dive.

As I pushed him out of the way, I yelled over the roar of automatic fire, "Get out there and fight or get the fuck out of the way!"

I then sprinted toward the irrigation ditch in front of the compound. As the bullets whizzed by me, I flipped off the safety on my M203. Then I dove into the ditch, firing an HEDP into the tree line just before landing. As I took up a stable position and started to reload my M203, Nolan plopped down beside me in the ditch and started firing his M4. Just as he did, rounds started to hit a few meters in front of me. Realizing how close the rounds had come to us, I turned toward Nolan to see if he had been hit. I then watched in amazement as he fired his M4 with his eyes closed. To make matters worse, he was firing his weapon without even having it shouldered! It was his shots that were hitting the ground right in front of me! I just shook my head, fired the HEDP I had just reloaded, and emptied my M4 into the tree line where the enemy fire was coming from.

Once my M4 ran dry, I took a knee behind cover to reload. As I pulled a fresh magazine out of my plate carrier, I heard someone yelling a very familiar phrase.

"Roadhouse!"

I knew this could be none other than the man himself, Sergeant Young. After I slammed a new magazine in my M4, I took a second to see what kind of badassery he was getting himself into. He was posted up at the end of the irrigation ditch with Murphy, who was on the M240B. Sergeant Young was standing completely upright and firing his M203 on cyclic like the hard-dick gunfighter he was. In between strings of HEDP, he was launching smoke grenades and directing Murphy on the M240B. He was effectively creating a lose-lose situation for the Talibros. By having Murphy pin the enemy down, he was making it easy for himself to engage the enemy with his indirect-fire weapon system: the M203 can fire at an arch and come down on top of an enemy who is stationary behind cover. Seeing this convinced me to switch back to my M203 and join in on all the fun.

Back inside the compound, Townsend was frantically trying to decide where to go or what to do.

Seeing this, Staff Sergeant Alonzo yelled, "Townsend!" Then, in a smooth calm voice, he said, "Town-

Sergeant Young in the ALP station that we secured in Gundi Ghar (courtesy Brandon Young).

send, calm down. We are being ambushed on all four sides. I need you on that roof right there, facing east."

Staff Sergeant Alonzo was on his fifth deployment and literally was as calm as I am when I check the mail. He was a super-professional soldier and perhaps the fittest human being I have ever met in person. He never got excited about anything, and we were lucky to have him in our platoon.

After being calmed down by Staff Sergeant Alonzo, Townsend made his way over towards the roof. Now he will tell you that he then jumped up, grabbed the wall, and pulled himself up on the roof. He knows that he used his superior athletic ability to accomplish this feat. Lemmon, however, seems to remember Townsend using his grizzled chin as a stepladder to get up there. The truth may never be known.

On the other side of the compound, Denton and DC saw some Taliban dude jump on a motorcycle and try to flee the fight yet again. Having decided that enough bad guys had escaped throughout the deployment, the two men turned both of their fully automatic weapons in his direction. They then simultaneously unloaded their M249s on the guy, killing him and his escape vehicle. They said they watched the motorcycle slowly roll away as the guy fell from it and it burst into flames.

Back out front, I was firing my M203 with reckless abandon while everyone around me did the same with whatever weapon was at their disposal. It wasn't long till we had the enemy on the run. This was the first time they had attacked us as an entire platoon and the firepower we had combined was much more than they had expected.

As the enemy fled and the firing died down, we could see a few Taliban fighters running across the open field with their AKs still in their hands. They were about 600 meters away and well beyond the range of my weapon systems. There were still guys with M4s trying to hit them, but to no avail. As I was watching them through my scope, I heard a loud single shot and watched one of them fall to the ground. I had forgot about Harris, the Platoon Designated Marksman with the M14! After seeing his compatriot fall, the second man started to move with a real sense of purpose, which caused Harris to miss with his next two shots. As the Taliban fighter was almost out of sight, I watched him ever so closely through my scope, hoping that Harris would connect before he made his escape. With the next shot fired, the man hit the ground and never stood up again. He was either smart enough to stay down, or else Harris had connected. I like to think the round found its mark.

With the firefight now over, most of us moved back inside the compound, leaving only necessary security personnel in position outside. As

11. Gundi Ghar, Day Two

I came back into the compound's courtyard, I saw Swoyer, our duck-billed battle puss, fumbling with his rifle. It was jammed and he couldn't seem to clear it. At this point in the deployment, I had pretty much decided that this was what the M4 was supposed to do. Upon further inspection of his ejection port, I got my first glimpse at the infamous bolt override.

Apparently, during the firefight, he had gotten an empty cartridge somehow seated above the gas tube of his M4. Malfunctions with the M4 are very common—I know, because I have had my share. I could go on and on about the weapon's lack of reliability. This malfunction, however, was different. This was one for the record books and I could not even fathom how it had happened. To make the situation even more ridiculous, during the firefight he had taken his rifle to the PL. He was directing the gunfight when Swoyer had asked him to fix his rifle. After some ten people had tried to fix the problem, the PSG took a look at it. Holding the bolt back with one hand, he slapped the charging handle forward, causing the round to fall right out. As he handed the rifle back to Swoyer, he explained that this wasn't the first time he had a special kid in his platoon.

While we were working on Swoyer's rifle, we found out that the HLZ that we had fought so hard for was of no use to us now. Higher command had denied our request to MedEvac Sanders. The company commander in charge literally said over the radio that he can walk out, or you guys can carry him out, but we aren't sending any more birds today. Mad as hell, we prepared to finish the operation with or without the support of higher command.

These new developments prompted us to have Second Squad take the lead and clear a path to the final compound. While they did that, we would maintain security in our current location and prepare to move the heat-injured soldiers. All this bad news in mind, the final objective for the day was only 800 meters away. So I was pretty sure we could get there even if it took the rest of the evening.

* * *

Two hours after heading out, Second Squad returned to our location. They had created a safe path through the IEDs and grape rows that would lead to our final compound for the day. Miraculously, Sanders was now conscious and able to walk. Doc Gio had given him at least a half-dozen IVs and had him stripped down naked at one point to cool off. We decided that everyone would take a portion of his gear, so that he could carry just an empty rucksack. He had the entire packing list for us to divvy up among ourselves. It was almost nonsensical the amount of equipment the PSG had put on that thing. As we handed out his equipment, I was thankful that my squad had decided not to carry the whole list. I am certain that I would have gone down myself if we had.

After exiting the compound, we entered the irrigation ditch I'd found myself in earlier that day. One hundred meters later, we climbed out of ditch and headed into a set of grape rows. Given the number of enemy personnel in the area, we wanted to stay as close to cover as possible. Up ahead of me, I could see a few guys securing the corner of the grape rows for us. As I passed by them, I realized it was Townsend and his fire team. As I nodded to Townsend, I couldn't help but notice that it looked as if he had been undressed. Perplexed but pressed for time, I kept moving without asking why. Later, Townsend told me that he'd started to pass out in the heat while waiting for us to come by. In a last-ditch attempt to escape the heat, he took off his helmet, unlaced his boots, threw his ruck to the side, undid his top, and tried to crawl under the low-hanging grapes in the row for what little shade they provided. He said he tried to sink into the mud like a burrowing toad. While he was under the grapes baking, he thought back to what I had said about the little rucksack, and how I had brought so little compared to him. He thought about how he told me I would regret bringing so few items on the packing list. "That fucking asshole was so smart to not bring all this stupid shit," he thought.

Deployment taught us something interesting about the heat and physical fitness. The guys who couldn't run before we left for deployment never had any problems rucking all day. Swoyer and Rodriguez fell out of almost every pre-deployment training run we'd done in the States. The both of them were, of course, endlessly belittled for it as well. Oftentimes, they were told that they were weak pieces of shit and that they would be the reason that others died. Reality proved to be quite different, however, as once we were in theater, those two guys never had any problems with the heat. They even ended up carrying all our so-called tough guys' equipment on more than one occasion. This just goes to show the lack of adequate training that we'd had before leaving for Afghanistan, as well as the lack of understanding as to what type of training is essential for success.

Shortly after we passed Townsend, we made our way to the last compound for the day. The rest of the element came in behind us safe and sound. We set up security and prepared for some much-needed rest. The following day, we'd still have a few more kilometers to cover before we reached the ANA checkpoint and our ride home.

The next morning as we prepared to move out, I realized just how tired everyone was. There was no talking, no laughing, just the blank stares of

11. Gundi Ghar, Day Two

very tired men. Everyone only did what he was told, then sat back down and waited for the next order. Considering that we were only about two kilometers from the ANA checkpoint, I was pretty sure that everyone would be able to make it.

Once all the preparations were made, the platoon stepped off toward our final destination. Lemmon cleared the way using the Mine Hound, with me close behind watching his six. As we moved along the grape rows that separated us from our final objective, the area looked almost peaceful. All I could see were a few local kids shooting slingshots. All I could hear was the call to prayer from a nearby mosque. Glancing over Lemmon's shoulder, I could just barely make out an Afghan flag placed atop a makeshift flagpole. That black, red, and green banner blowing in the breeze marked the end of a very long three-day weekend.

Once inside the checkpoint, everyone passed out on the ground wherever they could find space. There was no yelling from leaders, no orders being given, just the relief of a difficult mission completed. As everyone lay in the dirt next to the concrete walls of the ANA checkpoint, the PSG went around shaking everyone's hands.

"Good job out there, Roger," he said shaking Lemmon's hand. "Even you, Swoyer. You did pretty good," he said as he headed toward Odinson.

"You know who is not going to get a handshake today, Swoyer?" Lemmon asked with a smile.

"Who's that?" Swoyer asked, not sure what Lemmon was getting at.

"That bitch-ass cracker Sullivan who stayed back at Nalgham with a tummy ache!" Lemmon said as he and Swoyer laughed.

While the PSG shook hands, the PL explained that prior to this mission he had talked to some other officers who had tried to take units through this exact area in the past. He stated that they had met heavy resistance, and none had really been able to rout the enemy as we did—at least, not without losing a few soldiers. Thus, he felt that we had done pretty well under the circumstances. The Army is not big on compliments, but between the PSG's efforts to be personable and the PL explaining the true gravity of the situation, I felt like someone actually appreciated our efforts.

Speaking of the PSG, that one moment of normalcy that he had displayed made me see him in a completely different light. At the beginning of the deployment I would have told you that he was an idiot or maybe just a maniac. Some days I thought that he had just been in the Army way too goddamn long. Now I was starting to think it was something completely different. This was his last deployment! If he could survive this shit show he could go home, draw his pension and never deploy again. All he had to do was keep the Army from killing him one more time! He was hyper vigilant because he was going to make it home and he wasn't going to let a dumbass like me screw it up for him. This didn't make me suddenly like him, but I could sympathize with his position. I had only been in the Army for two and a half years and I couldn't wait to get out. I can't imagine how crazy I would be after twenty years of this bullshit.

As I lay in the dirt waiting for the trucks, I could not help but think about the day before and what the PL had told us. When it was all said and done, some part of the platoon had been under fire for ten straight hours. We had finally gotten what we all had asked for, what we had all joined for. Whether it would go on to haunt us, or be the greatest day of our lives, was yet to be known, but we had gotten what we asked for.

– 12 –

Chapman

The next day, I woke up to the recently promoted Staff Sergeant Hunter calling me and Sergeant Young out to the back of our tent for a meeting. Once there, Staff Sergeant Hunter explained that we were going to have a new guy added to our squad. We could tell by the apprehension in his voice that he felt like this guy was going to be a problem. Come to find out our new addition was recently demoted from sergeant to specialist. So he was going from being a squad leader to a SAW gunner. Staff Sergeant Hunter didn't know why he had been demoted, only that there had been 13 article 15s in the platoon he was coming from. Staff Sergeant Hunter didn't care what he had done, only how he was going to fit into the squad. He didn't want a former squad leader talking back to his team leaders or telling the other guys in the squad what to do. Staff Sergeant Hunter made it very clear that he didn't want us to give him any shit. He just wanted us to treat him like he acted. If he did his job, we were to leave him alone; if he turned out to be a fuckup, we would deal with him as we deemed fit.

That day went on as they usually did, with guard shifts and presence patrols. Just as I'd finished my guard shift and was headed toward my tent, I saw Staff Sergeant Hunter walking toward it. Next to him was a man who very strangely resembled Mega Mind. I got to the door just before the two of them, held the door open, then followed them in. Once inside, I threw my kit on my bunk. Staff Sergeant Hunter then called the squad to the center of the tent to introduce the man with the big head. As he presented the infamous Chapman, I reached out and shook his hand. At first glance he seemed like a perfectly reasonable troop to me.

Chapman was a very well-spoken fellow who we would find out later had a wealth of knowledge about the Army and the Infantry. Chapman was easygoing and for the most part made life much easier for those around him. He had had just a little too much fun in Third Platoon. After everyone had introduced themselves, we were all just kind of standing there waiting to hear what he had done to get demoted.

"Soooo? What happened?" asked Bertelli.

"Oh, you know, the usual—drugs, waterboarding, hazing, and assaulting Afghans. What can I say? We like to party in Three Chuck," Chapman laughed.

As we were all laughing, the PSG barged into our tent and ruined the mood. One of the ALP checkpoints was under attack and we needed to grab our gear and head to the trucks now! As he ran out, leaving the door open, Staff Sergeant Hunter gave us the hand-and-arm signal to kit up. I threw my gear back on, grabbed my rifle, and headed for the trucks. All of First Squad were at the vehicles within a few minutes, mounted up and ready to go. Right behind us followed Odinson's squad, who were also kitted up and ready to rock and roll.

As he was throwing in a huge lipper, Odinson came over to me to see if I knew what was going on. Come to find out we had both received the same detailed mission brief from the PSG by way of angry yelling. Why either of us thought the other should have any idea what was going on is unknown to me. It was our job to be uninformed, for the most part. After we finished laughing about how little the other knew, he climbed into his vehicle and I headed to mine. Rarely, if ever, were these quick-reaction missions anything real, but you never know. I then climbed into the passenger side of the mine roller and we were out the gate and headed to an ALP checkpoint. We didn't have far to go, since our destination was just a few miles down the road.

En route, the PL briefed us over the radio. He explained that the ALP checkpoint had been attacked and that we were going to do a battle damage assessment. Hearing this, Blackman turned towards me from the driver seat and rolled his eyes. Clearly, he wasn't thrilled that we had woken him up just to go see how fucked-up a bunch of ALP guys had gotten. I, on the other hand, kept my eyes peeled, as we had no idea what to expect until we got there.

As we arrived, we circled the wagons in a defensive perimeter around the checkpoint. It was only about the size of a small house with fifteen-foot-high walls, four towers, and one entrance. As Blackman parked our truck off the corner nearest the entrance, I could see one body lying on the ground just inside. Once all trucks were in position, everyone but the drivers and gunners dismounted. Without being given an order, everyone instinctively formed up and we moved toward the checkpoint. As I found my place in the formation that was stacking up on the entrance, Staff Sergeant Hunter got my attention with a hand-and-arm signal. He wanted me to stay with the trucks in case we needed someone to direct their movement while they were inside the checkpoint. This, of course, pissed me off to no end, as I was hoping to stack up on the door with the rest of the TCs. Nevertheless, I did as I was told, and ran back to my vehicle to rejoin Blackman. After a few minutes in which no enemy personnel were found in the area, the all-clear came over the radio.

"At least we didn't miss anything," I said to Blackman.

"Fuck, I don't care to get out of this truck, myself," Blackman said as he ate another mouthful of Skittles.

"I guess now we just wait," I said, shrugging my shoulders.

"You mean now we listen to our favorite jam, 'Call Me Maybe'!" Blackman yelled as he pulled out his .mp3 player.

As Blackman and I were jamming out to our favorite song, Lemmon reached down from the gunner's turret and kicked Blackman on the shoulder. "Crank that shit up, cracker!" he yelled excitedly.

After a considerable amount of time, some of the ALP commanders from nearby checkpoints started showing up to see what was going on.

"Nice of these guys to finally show up," Blackman said as they trickled in from the road.

"Yeah, it sure took them a long time to get here, considering that they are a lot closer than we are," I said as I looked out the window.

As Blackman and I were commenting on the punctuality of the ALP, Staff Sergeant Hunter opened the door on my side of the truck. He had a situation update for us. All seven of the Afghan Police officers were dead. Staff Sergeant Hunter explained that it looked like someone had killed them in their sleep. There was no sign of who did it at this point. Apparently, the ALP commanders who had arrived were doing nothing to help, either. Staff Sergeant Hunter told us that they were getting high and laughing at a stray dog that was splashing around in the blood. You could tell by the look on his face as he explained it that he was disgusted with their behavior. At this point in the deployment I was only half surprised by their antics. We had seen them do crazier shit, that's for sure.

"I will never understand these savages," Staff Sergeant Hunter said as he jumped down from the truck.

Once on the ground, he directed me to uncircle the wagons and get them on the road in order of movement. As Staff Sergeant Hunter closed the door, I pointed at Blackman and he threw the MATV in gear. While

Blackman wheeled the mine roller around, I got on the radio and called for the other trucks to follow suit. No sooner had we got into the order of movement than everyone was loaded up and we were headed back to COP Nalgham.

Later the next day, we found out that a man, who was possibly Taliban, had been for some time trying to steal that particular police chief's chai boy. After a few failed attempts, he resorted to drastic measures. He came by the checkpoint that night and got all the members baked and waited for them to pass out. He then proceeded to murder them all in their sleep and then take the chai boy for himself. Apparently, he then disappeared from the face of the earth, never to be seen again.

This is one aspect of the Afghan culture that is extremely hard for Americans to understand. The men, especially, are quite different from American dudes. The fact that many of these guys are pedophiles is very difficult for us to reconcile in any kind of moral way. Not only do the men in southern Afghanistan keep young boys around to sleep with, it is actually a point of prestige. The only thing I can liken it to in the United States is it's like having a trophy wife. The Afghan men will show off their chai boy to other leaders so as to display their status within the community. The higher status a tribal leader has, the better-looking and younger his chai boy will be. As shown above, the Afghan men often times kill each other over these chai boys. To make matters worse, the young boys themselves are oftentimes killed for various reasons. We ran into this practice almost daily when we worked with the ALP or ANA, but this case stands out in particular to me.

– 13 –

The Return to Gundi Ghar

We were tasked with returning to Gundi Ghar again in early July. Our mission was to remove several trees and terrain features that the Taliban had been using to conduct ambushes on 2–321. For this operation, we had one squad of our infantry guys, one squad of engineers, and an EOD team, totaling roughly thirty men. The engineers were going to do the actual demo work while we secured the area, whereas EOD was there to deal with the IEDs, of course. This was our fourth time going to Gundi Ghar and several of the guys were not happy about it. We were super close to the end of our tour and they didn't want to get killed a month before we all went home. I didn't really mind doing these missions; they were much better than standing in the guard towers and doing counter–IED patrols.

We arrived at a small checkpoint just outside Gundi Ghar the night before the mission. By this time in the deployment, this was standard operating procedure for operations in the AO. We made final preparations and got as much sleep as we could before waking up first thing in the morning. We hoped to beat the heat by leaving right at sunrise. The thirty of us exited the checkpoint in the standard file formation that we had become accustomed to. The minesweepers had a very busy day as they found IED after IED, making progress extremely slow. By the time we had made it to our objective area, the minesweepers and EOD had disposed of at least twelve devices. That's not counting the suspected IEDs we found and decided it best to just mark and go around. The number of devices in total far exceeded what we were accustomed to finding in a given mission, even for this IED-heavy AO. This meant that our marking chalk was running dangerously low. To make matters worse, we had not even started the demo work that was our actual mission.

Now at the designated area, with the trees that needed to be removed, we fanned out slowly and deliberately to set up security. A minesweeper, Bertelli, and I were charged with clearing out a few overwatch areas on the north side of the objective. These areas would provide us with the ability to keep the engineers safe while they worked. One look at the minesweeper's lazy gait and empty gaze was all it took to realize he was exhausted. He had been sweeping all day, and as a result was not doing a very good job searching for mines. This prompted me to request a new minesweeper so that the tired soldier could rest. Unfortunately, they sent up Wilson, who was even more exhausted than the guy who had been sweeping previously. He was lackadaisically swinging the Mine Hound back and forth while he curiously looked in all directions, which meant he was barely paying attention to what he was doing. Even after I yelled at him for his lack of concentration, his sweeping did not seem to improve.

So I stopped him, looked him in the eyes and said, "Wilson, we are counting on you, dammit!"

Nevertheless, he continued with the same half-ass sweeping despite my urgings to consider the team and not just himself. I have found that if people will not do something for themselves, they will almost never do it for someone else. As we continued following our professional mine sweeper, Bertelli called the team to a halt. He then pointed to a perfectly square discoloration in the dirt just about twelve inches from his right foot. Furious that Wilson had missed a perfectly visible IED, I stood there for a moment, shaking my head in disappointment. I decided that the best course of action was for us to use the footprints we had left in the moon dust to move back to safety.

Ever so slowly we walked backwards, being careful to stay in our own tracks, since we knew that they were clear. All I could think was that I had literally done this in video games before: traced my own steps in order to avoid stepping on a landmine.

Once we were a safe distance back from the discoloration, I called for EOD. They came right up, grabbed the Mine Hound from Wilson, and confirmed that it was indeed an IED. These guys were not our usual EOD team. I remember Staff Sergeant King saying that his team was very conservative and safe compared to the other teams in the area. I was about to see what he meant firsthand. With that thought fresh in mind, I watched as one of the EOD guys got down on his knees in front of the device. He then took two deep breaths while his buddy who was standing over him prepped his watch.

"Just say when, man; say when," the standing man said.

Then, after one final breath, the man in front of the device said, "Go!"

13. The Return to Gundi Ghar

His buddy clicked his watch and repeated, "Come on, come on, I got a minute forty-five earlier."

Bertelli just watched, stunned; he couldn't believe that they were timing it. The EOD guy working on the device pulled some wires, found a battery, disconnected it and threw it to the side, pulled and prodded on a few more parts, then threw his hands up like he'd just roped a cow.

"Done," he said.

"Minute thirty-seven, you bastard," said the guy holding the watch.

"I told you I was going to beat your weak-ass time," said the kneeling man as he wiped his brow.

They then had a good laugh and walked away like nothing out of the ordinary had happened. With the IED taken care of, the three of us moved on to our intended destination and set in security. I then called for the rest of our team to move down the path to help us secure the overwatch position. Once there, we watched as the engineers blew up trees and eliminated debris as fast as the minesweepers could clear the ground in front of them. Due to all the sweeping, the minesweepers had almost completely run out of chalk. They had even been mixing what little they had left with the moon dust to make it last as long as possible.

This prompted the PL to call higher command and tell them we may have to end the mission early. He explained that he felt it was unsafe to continue with no marking chalk and so many IEDs in the area. Higher command demanded that we figure it out. The PL tried to tell them that we could easily come back tomorrow to finish, but they didn't want to hear it. They told him that we would not leave until the mission was complete. I will never understand why a guy in an air-conditioned room has more authority than the ground force commander. Decisions like these should be at the discretion of the highest-ranking soldier on the ground.

This problem led us to improvise. We started to mark our paths with whatever we could find in our kits. First, we used our bright orange signal panels known as VF17. We cut them into long strips so that they could be set on each side of the cleared path, effectively creating a runway. Once we'd used all our panels, we became a little more desperate. The path was then marked with empty water bottles, pieces of MRE packages, and chem lights. We looked like a bunch of litterbugs throwing garbage everywhere we went. I was furious that higher command was willing to risk lives just to cut down a few trees today instead of tomorrow. I never really had a say in anything I did while in the Army, but this call made me particularly angry. Angry or not, I continued to pull security in my little corner of Afghanistan, just waiting for something terrible to go wrong.

As I sat in my corner and waited, I became increasingly bored, as did those around me. All that I had to entertain me were the local kids who were playing with slingshots and begging us for pens. The children in Afghanistan are relentless in their pursuit of the ballpoint pen. I have no idea what they use them for: I never saw a single piece of paper in Afghanistan, nor are many if any of them literate. Nevertheless, everywhere we went, there was at least one child yelling, "*Qalam raka*," which roughly translates to "give me a pen."

While we were battling off boredom and Afghan children, an interesting call came over the radio. We were told that a suicide bomber had been spotted in the area. He was wearing a blue man-dress, was clean-shaven, and had been instructed to head to our location. We were subsequently given orders to kill anyone dressed in this manner on sight. Now that there was a chance we might get to shoot someone, everyone was awake and on high alert. I scanned the area in front of me intently for about fifteen minutes before I gave up. Deciding that he wasn't coming, I returned to the slow bored gaze I had been using for the last several hours. Just as I gave up on a dramatic entrance from our suicide bomber, I heard two Apaches come overhead. Once on station they told us that they had spotted our man in the blue pajamas. He was north of our position and headed our way. I couldn't believe that he was actually going to try to make it to our location. North of our position meant that Lemmon would be on the side that the blue-dress bomber reached first. I was certain Lemmon was scanning his ass off right now waiting for this guy to show up.

Just as I suspected, Lemmon was scouring the long road in front of him leading toward the north. While he was glassing the edges of compounds, he spotted a man in a blue dress peering around the corner of a mud hut. Lemmon estimated that the blue-pajama bomber was just a short 100 meters ahead of him, an easy shot. Lemmon then flipped the selector switch on his rifle to fire and waited for the suicide bomber to expose himself again. At the exact moment the bomber stepped out into Lemmon's reticle, a massive roar of fully automatic fire rang out overhead.

Not knowing where it came from, everyone dove for cover. I immediately ducked down behind the small wall in front of me. As I raised my rifle up over the kalat wall, I could feel one of the Afghan kids clinging to my leg in an attempt to take cover. Seeing me dive into action, the PL started laughing and shaking his head. He was just standing in the open without a care in the world. Unbeknownst to me, one of the Apaches had informed him that they were about to engage our man in the pajamas. Since the rest of us hadn't been let in on this secret, we all dove into action

13. The Return to Gundi Ghar

when the Apache opened up with the .50 cal. After I composed myself, I was glad that someone got the bastard. All too often these guys get away and we are left with a bad taste in our mouths.

Almost immediately after the suicide bomber was shot, two men with a wheelbarrow ran out to his location. They picked up what was left of him, threw it in the wheelbarrow, and hauled ass out of there. They may not be pretty, but Afghan CASEVAC is quick. "Well, they definitely know we are here and they are making moves on us," I thought.

After the excitement died down, we returned to scanning while the engineers went back to work on the trees. Due to the brutal Afghan heat, the engineers had been rotating their men on a work/rest cycle for most of the day. Since Staff Sergeant Barns and Private Callen had been running a chainsaw for the last few hours, it was their turn to take a break in the shade. The only shady spot for miles was the corner of a small mud hut where Cristo, Lemmon, and Sanders had been pulling security. After handing the chainsaw off to another engineer, Staff Sergeant Barns and Callen headed toward the corner to escape the unrelenting sun.

Callen took refuge in the shade just a few steps in front of Staff Sergeant Barns. Once there, he threw his rucksack on the ground and stretched his back. When Staff Sergeant Barns reached the shade, he picked a comfy spot and slowly started to take a seat. Cristo could tell that the heat had taken its toll on the two men.

"You guys want to share some of this shade?" Callen asked Cristo as he leaned against the wall of the compound

"Get on in here, men," Cristo said with a smile.

Just as Cristo and Callen made eye contact, Staff Sergeant Barns came to rest on the pressure plate of an IED underneath him. This was followed by a deafening explosion and a blinding cloud of earth and debris. The force of the blast blew both of Lemmon's contacts out of his eyes and his dip down his throat! As the smoke cleared, the first thing that Cristo saw was Sanders on one knee staring motionless at the ground in front of him. Cristo slowly followed Sanders's line of sight to what had transfixed his gaze. There, just a few feet in front of him, was what was left of Staff Sergeant Barns. The force of the blast had completely disintegrated the lower portion of his body, leaving only torso and above intact. As those nearby realized what had happened, they opened fire on some Afghans in the adjacent field.

This was followed by men calling out "MEDIC!" and "CONTACT!" while others screamed for situation reports: "SITREP NOW!"

After hearing the calls for a medic, Doc Gio came running by me toward the men who were screaming for help. I still couldn't see what had happened, since there was a building between me and the blast. A few short minutes after Doc Gio had rounded the corner, I heard him yelling my name.

"Summerfield!" he yelled.

As I turned toward the sound of his voice, I could see that he was dragging behind him what was left of Staff Sergeant Barns.

"Summerfield!" he yelled again.

I had the backup litter on my kit. So if a medic was yelling my name, he must have more than one casualty.

"Summerfield, get over here!" he yelled.

As I ran over to his location, he lay Staff Sergeant Barns down and asked, "Take him to the clearing on your litter, would ya?"

"Roger," I said as I watched him run back to the blast area.

As I undid the litter from my kit, I knew someone else must be on the primary stretcher. They wouldn't ask for mine unless there was more than one casualty. While I unrolled the litter, I couldn't help but wonder who else was hurt. After I laid the litter out next to Staff Sergeant Barns, I yelled at two of the nearby engineers to help me set him on it.

"Hey, help me out!" I yelled.

They must have been in shock, because they did not respond to anything I said. Thankfully, Douglas came running up to my aid. A few feet from me, Douglas froze for a second and stared at the body of what used to be a soldier.

Seeing it stopped him where he stood, so I grabbed Staff Sergeant Barns's hand and said, "Let's do this!"

With that, we set him on the litter and moved him a short distance to where Doc Gio had directed me. Just as I was heading back to help at the blast site, Staff Sergeant Hunter yelled, "The medics got it under control. Fill in this hole in security."

As I took a knee in my security position, Doc Gio and another medic came by with what was left of Callen on a litter. He had not survived the blast either. From the looks of the two men, they had died instantly, which in a sad way is a good thing. If you have to go, painless is best. Cristo, Lemmon, and Sanders had only survived due to the fact that it was a directional IED. This means that the IED was constructed in a manner that the blast is funneled in a specific direction. Even though the three men were just as close to Staff Sergeant Barns as Callen, the blast was not channeled in their direction, leaving them relatively unhurt.

During the commotion, someone had called up on the radio that we had been hit with a recoilless rifle and not an IED. This meant that the MedEvac helicopters would not land till we had taken it out or the enemy had fled the area, since a recoilless rifle could be directed at the incoming birds. The PL kept trying to correct the error so we could get these two men on a chopper, but higher command thought he was trying to trick them into landing in a hot zone. The confusion delayed the MedEvac for hours. So all we could do was wait in the open exposed until the birds came.

After a somber five hours of waiting, we could hear the faint sound of rotors off in the distance. Once the birds came into sight, a purple smoke grenade was thrown out to mark the HLZ for the pilots. As the helicopter hit the ground, it pushed the smoke across the HLZ with its blades. Then several men ran two litters through the purple haze toward the chopper. After the two engineers were loaded up onto the bird, the radio crackled.

"Hero Bird, inbound. I say again, Hero Bird, inbound, over."

MedEvacs like these are called Hero Birds because they no longer transport casualties; they transport Heroes who have sacrificed it all. As the helicopter gained altitude, it pulled the last of the purple smoke up behind it. Ever so slowly, the Blackhawk faded away into the last remnants of light the day had to offer, leaving us behind to watch the Heroes ride off into the sunset.

As the sound of the birds faded away, we prepared for the long movement back to the trucks. For us, the mission was not yet over. We formed up into a long file, ensuring we kept five meters in between each man and the next. We did not want one IED to take out more than one man again that day. Since we had exhausted all of our impromptu marking materials, it was nearly impossible to mark areas swept by the Mine Hounds now. With no way to mark a cleared path, we resorted to walking in the footprints of the man in front of us. Under night vision, we walked slowly and meticulously. We had found several IEDs that day, and what happens if you set one off was fresh in our minds. I know I made certain to pay close attention to where the man in front of me was stepping as I trudged along.

After about an hour of walking, the man in front of me passed back the order to get nut-to-butt. Nut-to-butt is the eloquent way in which the Army asks everyone to close ranks. It means that everyone is to walk in a single file line, with each soldier as close to the man in front of him as possible. Even the silliest of paratroopers knows that you always keep your spacing. We already had too many near misses as a result of bad spacing this deployment, and I was not about to contribute to the problem. I was the fifth man in the line and was not going to be responsible for giving that order to twenty-six men in this IED-infested area. Seeing that I did nothing with the order, he passed it back again. I just looked at him like he was a moron and kept moving forward. I was certain that this was a mistake. There was no way that this actually came from anyone who mattered.

While I was marveling at this ridiculous idea, the PL came tearing down the line angrily. He was trying to figure out why no one behind me had closed in on the file. He whispered the order to me specifically, so he knew that I had received it. I didn't tell him no, but I didn't do it, either. I just kept my spacing. The PL ran all the way down the line telling each man individually to close ranks. As he came back up the line, he saw that I was literally the only guy that still had his spacing. So he got right in my face and told me to move it up.

"Why?" I said.

"We don't want to lose anyone in the dark," he said.

"Lose someone in the dark? What the fuck are we doing?" I asked myself.

My complaints and defiance had been for naught, as by this time the entire line had closed in on me. I was nut-to-butt now whether I wanted to be or not. Later, I would ask the PL about the order and he told me it had come from the man in the air-conditioned room, not him. He said he fought it harder than I did, but in the end had to do as he was told. I will never agree with the order, but I knew the PL to be a much better soldier than to have come up with that idea himself.

We moved on and on for another hour or so when we came to a field of rocks varying in sizes from softball to basketball size. Everyone was having an incredibly difficult time walking, and most were falling so often they resorted to crawling. The field was no longer than 100 meters, but it took almost a half an hour to cross. It was really just ridiculous. I have never had so much trouble walking in my life. Watching a bunch of infantrymen crawl on all fours during combat operations is about as demoralizing as it can get. Every ten feet or so I would get furious with crawling and try to stand up and walk, only to be further humiliated when I again fell and had to resume crawling like a baby.

Once we finally got out of the field of rocks, we were almost back to the checkpoint and finished with this absurdly long day. It had been just over twenty-two hours since we first stepped off to begin the patrol and I was extremely tired. I could see the trucks now and knew we would be back at our COP in less than an hour. All we had to do was cross a few grape rows and an irrigation ditch. Everyone was walking along when Staff Sergeant Hunter stubbed his toe on the tiniest root in Afghanistan. Unfor-

13. The Return to Gundi Ghar

tunately, that little root was on a downhill slope. It looked as if someone had picked him up and thrown him down the embankment. He hit the ground so hard and violently that I could not believe he hadn't broken any bones. It was both painful and hilarious. After a brief moment of reflection, he stood up, collected himself, and turned toward Lemmon. He looked him straight in the face and said, "Don't you laugh, asshole!"

"Negatron, Sergeant," Lemmon said in his casual tone, ensuring not to laugh.

I just kept my gaze on the ground, since I knew looking at him would cause me to lose what little composure I had left. After Staff Sergeant Hunter's cliff-diving exhibition, we continued to the trucks. Once there, I knew we were only a short fifteen-minute drive from COP Nalgham, and I was ready for bed.

As we pulled into the motor pool, Staff Sergeant Hunter said, "Don't fuel the trucks, don't clean them out, go to bed. We will take care of this shit in the morning."

I just grabbed my gear and headed straight to my tent. As I got to the door, there was the PSG yelling at guys and waving his arms around like a madman.

"Who was mine sweeping? Which one of you was it?" the PSG screamed at me.

I just walked past him. I couldn't believe that was the first thing he said when we got back. I went in the tent, threw my ruck on my shelf, hung my rifle on the cross post, kicked off my boots, and sat down on my bunk. As I was sitting there rubbing my eyes, Lemmon came and sat down next to me.

"They killed the fucking kittens," he said, looking at the floor.

"What?" I asked, confused. I was still focused on the PSG and his ridiculous question. Thus, I didn't quite take in what Lemmon had said.

"While we were gone, First Sergeant found out we had the kittens and he threw them in the burn pit," Lemmon said with a solemn look on his face.

"A-fucking-live?" I asked, even more confused.

"Fuck, yes, alive!" he shouted while throwing his hands in the air.

"Why the fuck did they do that?" I asked.

"DC told me that they said they could carry diseases, so they had to get rid of them," Lemmon explained.

"Diseases!" I said angrily as I lay down.

"Sorry, dude, I thought you would want to know," Lemmon said as he stood up and headed to his bunk.

As I lay there thinking about the totality of the day, I couldn't for the life of me figure out why they had burned them! We had five million bullets on the COP! It was somehow the last nail in the coffin of what had been an arduous ordeal. Looking around, you could tell that everyone felt pretty much the way I did about the day as a whole. After taking in the tone of the room, I rolled over and wrapped up in my sleeping bag. I fell asleep as soon as I closed my eyes, thus concluding the longest day of my life.

– 14 –

Back to the Grind

The day following the mission to Gundi Ghar, we returned to the grind of tower guard and presence patrols. At this point in the deployment, I was in charge of organizing guard and patrol shifts. So I started giving guys a break from the towers by trading them my ECP shifts for their shifts in the tower. The ECP was slightly better than the towers, since you were there with someone to talk to. That meant you didn't have to sit alone for six hours wishing a stray bullet would save you from the endless monotony, a boredom so severe it caused you to slowly slip into madness. Honestly, it was to the point of a nervous breakdown, after which you had to compose yourself and prepare to do it all over again. Despite the mental anguish of tower guard, we were within the last few weeks of the deployment. You could tell that everyone was more than ready to go home and never come back to this shithole country again.

I was standing in the northeast tower, staring into the abyss that was my security sector, when the call for a MedEvac came over the radio. I couldn't hear the entire transmission, which came in broken, but I did make out three words: "Green on blue." This meant only one thing: one of the damn ALP or ANA had shot one of our guys. Staff Sergeant Hunter had told us before we left the States to never fully trust the Afghans. He always made sure we kept our distance. Staff Sergeant Hunter made it clear we were not about making friends with the locals. He knew if we dropped our guard around them, they would be ready to shoot us in the back. I took this advice to heart and was always very wary when working around them. I never let myself forget what had happened earlier in the deployment with Bravo Company. Nevertheless, some of the guys became friendly with ALP and the ANA to the point that they would let their guard down around them.

The radio transmissions came in a few more times with no clear information. Confused and concerned, guys in the towers started calling up, trying to figure out who had been hurt. Despite their concerns, they were told to keep the line clear so that the birds could get through when they arrived. So all I was left with was waiting to see who had got hurt and how bad. I sat in the tower for the longest five hours of the deployment, hoping that whoever got hurt was all right.

After an eternity of waiting, my shift came to an end when one of the weirdos from our headquarters platoon came to replace me. He was fifteen minutes late, had his helmet on backwards, and his boots were untied. Since he was the first person I could ask about the green on blue, I hoped he would be able to tell me what had happened. Much to my dismay, he was completely oblivious to the fact that there had been an attack. He had been asleep all day and could not be bothered with such trifling matters. Enraged by his inability to do anything that even resembled soldiering, I pushed him out of the way and headed toward the door.

I hurried toward the center of the COP to ask someone who was not a complete moron what had happened. Some of the headquarters guys did almost nothing all day and would just pull random tower guard shifts once a week. It was really crazy, the disparity between who worked and who didn't. As I thought about the weirdo I'd left in a stupor in the tower, I made my way back to the tents. En route I ran into Chapman and Staff Sergeant Hunter—thankfully, two smart people in one place. "What luck," I thought. I couldn't ask them what had happened fast enough.

Chapman explained that during a joint ALP–Three Chuck patrol, one of the ALP guys asked Henderson if he could check out the scope on his rifle, which is something that they often do. What was not a normal occurrence was that Henderson decided to hand the man his rifle. As Chapman continued, I was pretty sure that I knew where this story was headed. Once Henderson was weaponless, the ALP dude waited for him to let his guard down. He then got behind him and shot him in the neck with his own rifle! Hearing this for a second time enraged Staff Sergeant Hunter for multiple reasons. First of all, he had been preaching not to trust these assholes since before we left the States. Second, they had managed to escape with his rifle, which was equipped with a night vision capable device.

I couldn't believe that the ALP guy managed to escape. In reality, I couldn't believe that Three Charles had left a single ALP guy standing. We would have just unloaded on every bad guy-shaped object in the general vicinity. To make matters worse, no one from Three Charles fired a single round. Much to Staff Sergeant Hunter's dismay, one of their M240

14. Back to the Grind

gunners just watched them escape towards the desert to the south. With all these confusing facts taken into consideration, it looked like Henderson was going to be OK. At the end of the day, that was the most important thing for all three of us.

Once they had given me the lowdown, I headed back to my tent, puzzled by the whole event. "Too many whys in this for me to ever understand it," I thought. At least we are out of this shitty country soon, just a few more weeks. As I contemplated the incident, I took off my kit, lay down, and then went to sleep.

* * *

A few hours later, I was woken up by Staff Sergeant Hunter to go replace Townsend in Tower Two.

"I think there is a mistake. I just got off guard like three hours ago, Sergeant," I said as I checked my watch, confused.

"Well, Townsend has been on guard for eighteen hours," said Staff Sergeant Hunter.

"Holy shit, OK. Well, here I go," I said.

I grabbed my gear, a few Rip Its, and a MRE, and made my way toward Tower Two. When I approached the tower, I saw a defeated man. He was just blankly staring off into the nothingness that was the desert in front of him.

"What's up?" I said.

"I... want... to... die..." Townsend slowly stammered.

"Holy shit. Why were you here so long?" I asked, looking him up and down.

"First Sergeant [1SG] made me stay here," he said with no intonation in his voice.

"Why is that?" I asked, knowing full well he must have fucked up something.

"I wasn't wearing my knee pads," he said, staring at his knees.

"Classic mistake," I said. "So how long have you been in this motherfucker? Sergeant Hunter said like eighteen hours."

"I don't know, but I have had a complete nervous breakdown and regained my composure like three times," mumbled Townsend.

"Really? Holy shit," I said, raising my eyebrows in disbelief.

"Yeah, I have been standing here smoking all the used cigarette butts on the floor and chewing the coffee grinds from the MRE packets that people left in this ammo can," replied Townsend as he looked through me.

"Jesus," I laughed.

"And I don't even smoke! I have just been doing all that I can to stay awake in this piece-of-shit tower," said Townsend.

"So, what exactly happened?" I asked.

Townsend explained that when he got into the tower, he took his knee pads off like he always does and put them on the shelf behind him. He then checked the sector sketches, started drinking his coffee, and pulled security just as happy as a clam. As he was standing there, someone snuck in behind him. When he turned around to see who it was, he saw 1SG standing in the entryway of the tower. He started asking Townsend questions about his security sectors, claymore positions, and weapon systems, all of which he got right. Then he looked at Townsend, and nodded as if to say not bad. 1SG then turned to exit the tower. Just as Townsend started to breathe a sigh of relief, 1SG's eyes stopped on the knee pads on the shelf. He then shifted his gaze from the pads to Townsend's bare knees. He freaked out, started screaming at him, and told him to go get the PSG. He said he would pull security in the tower till Townsend got back.

So Townsend had to go find the angriest PSG in town and tell him not only that he had fucked up, but that his boss wanted to see him. Not wanting to explain the situation to the PSG, Townsend told him that 1SG wanted to see him in Tower Two, then ran away. He did it so fast that he made it back to the tower before the PSG could ask him any questions. The PSG was hot on his tail, however, and showed up in the tower just after Townsend did. At that point, the two leaders united to let Townsend know how big of a piece of shit he was. Then the PSG told him since he was so comfortable in the tower that he thought he didn't need his knee pads, he could stay in it forever. He left Townsend in the tower for almost an entire day wishing for his demise. After his story, Townsend slowly made his way down the steps out of the tower. He had only one thing on his mind: his bed.

Tower guard is not that bad until you have done it for six to fifteen hours a day for six months straight. It becomes almost unbearable for some guys. It is incredibly boring and there is always someone sneaking around trying to catch you slacking on the job. It's just one of those thankless jobs that must be done. Later in my life when I got out of the Army, I literally turned down a hundred-thousand-dollar-a-year job because it consisted of twelve hours of tower guard a day. I'd literally rather work at a fast food place.

– 15 –

Deegan Cole

We conducted well over 100 mounted patrols throughout the deployment, most of which were uneventful and boring. There was a plus side, however, as I was usually in charge of planning who was in what truck. So I got to pick my drivers and gunners. I oftentimes picked good old DC to drive me; he rarely got our truck stuck and he was usually pretty fucking hilarious. However, he was prone to getting me into a little trouble from time to time.

On a particularly hot day in July, DC and I were tasked with driving the LMTV to an outpost construction site. The LMTV is a large up-armored flatbed truck. It has two seats in the front, three if you're desperate, and no turret. Thus, the LMTV always had to be accompanied by two escort vehicles for protection. We had loaded the LMTV down with Hescos, C-wire, and fence posts. We were to provide these supplies, aid the front-end loaders, and help the troops on the ground build an ALP checkpoint not far from our COP. Once we arrived on site, the PSG was already on the ground, throwing a fit and acting like the maniac he was.

Sizing up the situation, I motioned for DC to let me out so I could help him back up the LMTV. Our vehicle had only one functioning door on the driver side, so I had to crawl over DC to get out of the truck. It is Army standard to have the truck commander (TC)—me, in this instance—get out of the vehicle and guide the driver anytime he places the vehicle in reverse. Thus, like a good soldier, I was going to follow the rules.

Of course, DC was having none of the rules and said, "No, no, I got this, Summerhoss. You just relax. I don't need a ground guide."

"Let me out. The PSG is right there. He will smoke our balls off if we don't use a ground guide," I said.

"I'm a professional driver. I can do this, little buddy," DC said with a smile.

"You have to back a thirty-foot truck up around two corners, through moving people, across a bridge, and in between the two front-end loaders currently working on the checkpoint. There is no way!" I said.

"I got one good mirror on this bitch," DC said as he threw the LMTV in reverse.

"Oh no!" I said as I jumped in his lap and started to open the lock on the driver's door.

"I won't follow your directions even if you get out," DC said, laughing.

We fought over the combat lock for a bit before he realized I was starting to get pretty pissed. Deciding it wasn't worth the effort, he let me open the door and jump down. After I got out of the truck, I looked up at him and said, "Just follow my hand signals."

"Nope, no chance, Summerbreeze," he said.

"Jesus," I thought as I closed the door on the vehicle.

"What the hell is taking so long, Sammerson?" yelled the PSG.

"How the fuck does he still not know my name?" I thought. "Just fighting the broken doors, Sergeant," I said.

As usual, the PSG wasn't in the mood for my excuses and he had no qualms about hurrying me along. So, with some extra motivation, I rounded the front of the vehicle to where I could see DC. I looked up at him and gave him the signal to turn the truck to the left and go in reverse. He responded by shaking his head "no," like a three-year-old refusing to eat his vegetables. "Today is not the day for fucking games, DC," I thought, grinding my teeth. As I gave him the signal again, he pulled down the sun visor and shut his eyes. To be absolutely certain he could not see any signal I gave him, he then held his hand up in front of his already closed eyes. He then gunned the truck in reverse. The LMTV took off with reckless abandon! As he was careening into the unknown, I frantically signaled for him to turn to his left. All of a sudden, a huge crash brought his movement to a halt! I looked at DC and ground my teeth angrily. He knew he had fucked up because he took his hands off the steering wheel and pretended to pull his hair out. He was, of course, laughing at the situation at the same time. I just shook my head at him and headed to the rear to inspect the damage. "Goddammit, the PSG is going to freak out," I thought.

I went to the rear, where DC had run into one of the front-end loaders. He hit it hard enough that he'd wedged the LMTV under it, lifting one side of the tracks off the ground. The driver of the front-end loader was an Afghan local, and our interpreter Amardad was riding with him. They both looked at me trying to decide what to do when Amardad jumped down

15. Deegan Cole

from the unsteady vehicle. As he landed, I saw him grimace, since the wound he'd received on our first trip to Gundi Ghar had yet to fully heal.

"You ran into my guy!" Amardad yelled.

Not knowing what to say yet, I just yelled, "What?" over the engine noise.

"You hit my guy!" he yelled again.

"Your guy hit my guy?" I said.

"No, you hit my guy!" Amardad yelled.

"Oh no, you hit my guy!" I insisted as I waved DC to pull forward to set the vehicle back down on both tracks.

Amardad and I went back and forth a few more times as the PSG headed our way. Just as he arrived, the interpreter finally agreed that I was indeed right. Somehow, I had convinced him that the Afghan driver had hit my truck.

"What's going on here, Samsonite?" the PSG yelled at me.

"Oh, this Afghan hit DC as he was sitting here, Sergeant," I said.

The PSG then looked at Amardad for confirmation. Amardad slowly nodded his head yes, almost in disbelief. He then climbed on the loader with the driver and ushered him back to work. This, of course, meant that Amardad had now saved my ass twice.

The PSG and I walked around to the front of DC's truck as he said, "If these fucking Afghans would pay attention like you and DC, we would get a lot more done a lot faster."

"Indeed, we would, Sergeant," I said.

As I breathed a sigh of relief, I thought, "How do you know Deegan Cole's nickname and not my actual name?" When I reached the LMTV driver's door, DC and I quickly exchanged looks of disbelief. I could tell he was amazed that the PSG wasn't losing his mind. Without daring to ask for an explanation, DC let me guide him to the entrance so that we could unload the materials.

The construction continued late into the night. Our little three-vehicle convoy made trip after trip, back and forth from the COP to the checkpoint, bringing supplies. Blackman was driving the mine roller in front, D.C. and I in the middle, and the PL was pulling up the rear. This particular night was moonless and cloudy. To make matters worse, the LMTV had no blackout lights on it, which made the trip quite difficult. Blackout lights are infrared headlights that can only be seen with the use of night-vision goggles. This meant we could see them, but the enemy could not. The PL who was in the truck behind us had decided that we could not use our normal headlights, which would give our position away to the enemy. This was normally fine, but with no moon and no blackout lights, D.C. and I could barely make out the road in front of us, while the mine roller and the PL's truck had great blackout lights. Most of the trip between the checkpoint and the COP was flat and easy to drive, but there was a narrow bridge that traversed a seven-foot-deep dropoff. This was a difficult bridge to cross during the day, let alone under these conditions. So I called the PL as we approached to ask if we could use white lights to cross it. He felt that it was way too dangerous and he did not want us to risk it. Even after I tried to explain that we would switch back to blackout immediately after we crossed, he still wouldn't agree to it. DC was a damn good driver and half insane, and he still felt like it was a bad idea. There was barely a one-foot clearance on either side of the bridge and we could see almost nothing.

In my mind, the dangers of driving off this bridge, rolling the LMTV, stranding everyone out here for hours to get me and DC out of the truck, not to mention recover it, greatly outweighed the chance that we would be shot at in an up-armored vehicle during a ten-second light blast. While rationalizing my next decision, I did remember that I am barely in charge of when I go to the bathroom around here. Thus, the PL may not have been overly concerned with my decision-making process.

I asked one more time for white lights, just to be denied by a now noticeably angry PL. Starting to get pretty pissed off myself, I decided that we were using them. DC hit his lights just as we got to the bridge. When the beams lit up the road, we were dangerously close to it and hilariously off centered. DC threw the truck in reverse, corrected, and then proceeded across with no problem. Once across, he switched the lights off immediately. The light blast could not have lasted more than thirty seconds. This was way too long for the PL, who was now furious. He demanded an explanation over the radio as DC chuckled and fumbled with his iPod. I did not respond to him. "He can just be mad at me when we get there," I thought. After we pulled into the COP, the PL gave me the what-for. Fortunately for me, he was a reasonable man and I explained to him we could not see at all. He accepted my excuses but made it clear that I would not use my white lights on the way back.

After our talk, we loaded up the LMTV and prepared to head back to the checkpoint with the supplies. I tried to convince the PL to let me use the white lights one more time, but he was not having it. So, DC decided that he would try to stay right on the lead truck's taillights in hopes of not getting too far off the road. This seemed to work at first, but it eventually was all for naught, because Blackman was way too fast. He had brand-new blackout lights on the mine roller that lit the road up like it was daytime. When the mine roller crossed the bridge, Blackman took off, leaving us in the moon dust. After the mine roller's taillights disappeared, DC and I could see nothing but darkness. Knowing we were almost at the bridge, I had DC stop so that I could ask one more time about the goddamn lights.

"Permission to use white lights, over," I asked.

"Negative," replied the PL, noticeably annoyed.

I was starting to get pretty pissed myself. Not sure what to do, I looked at DC to gauge his reaction.

"Fuck it, bro. Let's just drive this motherfucker off a mountain," he said, shrugging his shoulders.

"Well, let's try to make it across, at least," I said as DC put the LMTV back in gear.

In typical DC fashion, he slammed it in gear and floored it. Just as I thought we were going to make it, we were airborne. DC had ramped the LMTV off the side of the bridge, and we were on our way straight to the bottom of the irrigation ditch! As we crashed into the bottom, all the loose equipment in the truck ricocheted around the cab violently. After all the moon dust had cleared, I came to realize that the truck was wedged at an angle between the bridge and the creek bottom. My side of the truck was almost completely blocked by rocks and debris. That wasn't too big of a deal because the door didn't work anyway. Since the PL was behind us, he must have seen the whole debacle unfold.

"Are you fucking serious?" said the PL over the radio.

"We can't see shit, over," I grumbled into the radio.

We were sitting there at a very precarious angle. It felt like we could roll over any second. All of the trucks are equipped with gauges that tell the driver when they are about to roll over. Knowing this, I looked around the cab to see how close we were to the danger zone. I wanted to see more to have a laugh than anything, since knowing how many degrees we were from tipping over wouldn't change anything now. Looking around, I could not seem to find the gauge anywhere. I was sure that the LMTV had one somewhere, though.

"Does this piece of shit have no gauge in it either?" I asked DC.

"No, no, here it is. That's where I hang my helmet, Summerhoss," DC said as he lifted his helmet off the gauge.

The gauge was maxed out at forty-eight degrees, which is well past the supposed rollover angle. We both laughed as I told him he better put his helmet back on before the PL saw him without it. After he slapped it on, the PL showed up in front of the truck. He was on foot and waving for

DC to turn his wheels away from the bridge. DC then cranked the steering wheel as fast as he could to the right. As he did, the truck rocked precariously, causing the chin strap on his helmet to swing back and forth wildly. "Holy shit!" I thought. "He didn't even bother to buckle the damn thing." The PL called over his portable radio for DC to gun it in reverse, and somehow the truck righted itself. Amazed that this had leveled us out, I sat back in my seat and breathed a sigh of relief. It took DC a few tries to get out of the creek bottom, but before we knew it, we were back on track and headed to the checkpoint with the supplies.

We arrived at the checkpoint at around 0300, and once we unloaded the truck, the PL decided to call it a night. As we prepared to move back to COP Nalgham, the PL called for all trucks to go white lights. This, of course, came as no surprise to DC, who was sitting in the driver seat laughing.

Once we got back to COP Nalgham, we fueled the trucks and headed to bed. I had been asleep for about an hour before I was woken up to go on guard duty at the entry control point (ECP). I begrudgingly gathered my gear, plus half a dozen Rip Its, and headed toward the ECP. Wondering who was on shift with me, I heard someone vomiting his guts up around the Hesco wall. As I rounded the corner toward the ECP, I could see good old Deegan Cole holding up an IV bag that was attached to someone in the Porta-John.

"Sommerhoss, good morning," he said with a smile.

"Who's that?" I asked.

"Why, of course, it's your buddy Big Town!" said DC, laughing.

The door was wide open to the Porta-John, and I could see Townsend sitting on the toilet. He was shitting his life away while he vomited into the urinal. Somehow DC still thought all this army stuff was funny.

– 16 –

The Complexities of My Emotions

Shortly after returning to the grind of force protection, our platoon was tasked with clearing out two small village sets to the southeast of COP Nalgham. This mission would consist of Third Squad and a squad of our partner forces from the Afghan National Army. They would be supported by a gun team comprised of Odinson, Staff Sergeant Alonzo and Thompson, as well as the ever-important three-man EOD detachment led by Staff Sergeant King. Their objective was to push into the two small villages in an attempt to probe the area for enemy forces. Before they left, the unit that we replaced warned us to stay out of this area. They explained that the one time they tried to push their way in they were met with heavy resistance, to the extent that they decided to abandon any hope of securing the area during their deployment. Despite their warnings, our overall mission was to take and control enemy terrain, so there was no way around it. One way or another, someone was going to have to swing on by and introduce themselves.

The morning of the operation, I woke up and was headed to the one place where I spent the majority of my time on deployment, the goddamn ECP. On my way I stopped by the supply tent to grab some Rip Its and a few MREs. Since half of the platoon was going to be out on a mission, the rest of us would be pulling double shifts of force-pro until they returned. After I grabbed my-life saving resources, I made my way to the ECP. The majority of Third Squad was already there, preparing to depart for a day of fun and adventure. I was to man the ECP with Lemmon that day, so I at least had good company. I don't know if I could handle throwing another 12 hours of my life away listening to Sullivan cry about going home.

After I took control of my post, I decided to mingle with the men who were about to leave. I wanted to judge the overall tone of the operation. Douglas and the PL were discussing target reference points, phase lines and air support. Staff Sergeant Alonzo and Odinson were drilling what they would do if they were to come under enemy fire. You could tell from the serious demeanor of the men that they were indeed expecting contact. It's crazy to think that they could get in that much trouble a few hundred meters from the COP. The first village was so close we could see it from the ECP.

As Third Squad formed up to move out, I could hear Odinson yelling at Wilson to get to the front of the file. He was lagging behind and needed to get ready to sweep with the Mine Hound. Wilson was a skinny kid, no more than 140 pounds. He was always in trouble with his team leader and was generally considered to be a below-average soldier. That said, he was a good dude with an unreasonably upbeat demeanor. He had no problem helping anyone out; he just couldn't seem to keep himself out of trouble. But he never let the pushups and the constant verbal attacks on his masculinity get him down. After Odinson yelled at him one more time, Wilson moved to the front of the formation. He made a half-hearted attempt to look like he was hurrying for good show. As they snaked their way out of the gate, Wilson looked back at me with a goofy smile and gingerly waved goodbye.

At 0800, Third Squad made their way down the road, meticulously sweeping for IEDs. Wilson pushed along, waving the Mine Hound back and forth as Sanders marked a safe path with chalk dust. At the same time, the rest of the men kept a sharp lookout for potential enemy personnel. The Afghan soldiers, on the other hand, wandered in and out of the safe area that had been marked by Sanders. The PL tried to convince his ANA counterpart that he needed to keep his men in the swept area, but his reply was all too telling.

"My men will find the IEDs with their feet. We don't need to wait on you," Commander Tabish said with a thick Dari accent.

We had about as much control over our local counterparts as they had over us. It might be better to describe our joint operations as simultaneous missions. From the outside it appeared more like two units running similar missions in the same general vicinity than it did two units working together. This meant that the Afghans were free to snake in and out of the safe zone as they deemed fit.

The element hadn't even reached the first compound on their list of objectives when Wilson found an IED buried just below the earth's surface.

16. The Complexities of My Emotions

Like they had done countless times before, Third Squad moved back, secured the area, and swept out security positions. This would allow them to watch over Staff Sergeant King and his team while they conducted a Blast in Place. After the BIP was completed, everyone listening to the radio was fully convinced that this was indeed as bad of an area as we had heard. Third Squad must have felt the same way, since they moved on afterwards much more deliberately. Slowly but surely, they pushed on toward the first compound that they needed to clear.

Everyone on guard duty listened intently to their radios and watched the element closely. With a fully functioning IED already in play, the mission could go sideways at any moment. Third Squad barely began setting security in the first mud hut on the left side of the road when Commander Tabish got his wish. As Wilson was sweeping his way around the structure, one of the ANA soldiers ran on up ahead of him and quite proudly took point. Pushing his way across an open field, he forged onward into unclear terrain. The very instance that he settled into his stride, he found what Tabish was looking for. Stepping down with his right leg, he placed all his weight on a makeshift pressure plate just below the earth's surface. Doing so closed a circuit that sent an electrical current to a detonator that set off the main charge of an improvised explosive device. The blast threw moon dust in all directions while the overpressure from the explosion stopped everyone dead in their tracks. It took only a few short seconds for the formation to realize what had happened. During that brief moment, the first sharp whizzes and zips of 7.62 started to make their way towards the guys in Third Squad. Every firefight seems to start with one zip, two whizzes, and then an overbearing pressure that comes from the deafening roar of two-directional automatic fire.

As the fire between the two elements came to a climax, the PL gave two quick commands. First, he wanted the main element to breech the mud hut with a red door just to the left side of the road. Second, he wanted Staff Sergeant Alonzo to take Odinson, Thompson and the M240B to a support-by-fire position on a nearby hill.

The three men stayed low and moved quickly to where the PL wanted the gun team emplaced. Once there, they got into a good position where they could lay down suppressing fire on known, likely and suspected enemy positions. Staff Sergeant Alonzo had found a well-fortified position behind a kalat wall that would provide good cover from incoming fire. As Odinson set his gun up, Staff Sergeant Alonzo noticed a boot lying on the ground next to him behind the wall. The IED blast had blown the ANA

Odinson manning the M240B position in the graveyard (Dick Mountain) (courtesy Brandon Young).

dude's boot a hundred meters from the X. Moving the boot around, he could feel something loose banging around on the inside. With a puzzled look on his face, he slowly tipped the boot upside down to see what it contained. Carefully pouring it out, he watched the ANA soldier's big toe roll out of the boot and onto the ground. Odinson could not believe that the boot had stayed intact and the foot didn't. Staff Sergeant Alonzo looked even more confused than Odinson as he set the boot to the side with an unwarranted level of care.

Their confusion was abruptly interrupted when direct and accurate fire started to rain down around the men. While rounds ricocheted and zipped off the kalat wall near Odinson, he could do nothing but hunker down and take cover. A sniper had taken up the perfect position, as he placed the main element in between himself and Odinson's M240. He knew all too well that the gun team would not fire for fear of hitting their own men. The sniper, on the other hand, couldn't care less if he accidently hit one American while shooting at another.

16. The Complexities of My Emotions

Back at the ECP, I could hear all the chaos but had no idea what was going on. I could tell friendly and enemy weapon systems were being fired and I heard an explosion, neither of which provided me with any information. Running through all of the possible scenarios in my mind of who was hurt and how bad was not doing them or me any good. The mind doesn't always drive one's thoughts in the best direction, though, does it? Unfortunately for me, my internal dialogue was interrupted by bad news as the PL came over the radio loud and clear.

"Suspected sniper position northwest of our current location over," the PL said in a perfectly calm command voice.

"Roger that, we'll try to obtain visual with tower cam, over," the TOC responded in a noticeably less calm manner.

"We need some air support over here as well, over," the PL explained, surprisingly calmer than the first transmission.

"I'll see what I can do," the TOC responded with some serious doubt in his voice.

"Great," I thought, these assholes are out here in a no-shit complex ambush. While they are fighting it out with every bad guy in Kandahar, I'm stuck here listening to them become a bunch of fucking war heroes.

As the PL clipped his radio back onto his plate carrier, he grabbed the Remington 870 from the man behind him. He then angled the muzzle of the breeching tool just off the red door's top hinge and pulled the trigger. The blast from the shotgun seemed to evaporate the cheap aluminum hinge that held the door in place. Then, in one motion, he racked the slide and fired a second round at the bottom hinge, rendering it as useless as the top one. The man behind him then took a quick stutter-step and kicked the door clean off its hinges. As the door crash landed on the floor and slid to a stop, Third Squad made entry into the small Afghan home.

"Go! Go! Go!" the PL yelled as Third Squad took the mud hut's courtyard by force.

The squad met no resistance as they cleared the interior and exterior rooms of the structure. Once the building was secure, they started to do their standard checks to ensure that all personnel and equipment were accounted for. Upon completion, they came to the realization that Wilson was missing. Sanders immediately flew into a rage. Of course, it was Wilson who was missing, he couldn't do anything right!

As everyone frantically began looking for him, Doc Gio spotted a lone soldier casually mine-sweeping his way across the same open field our ANA hero had proudly forged across just moments before. With enemy gunfire coming from what seemed like all directions, Wilson pushed out towards the injured man. He was ever so carefully using his Mine Hound to sweep a safe path to the fallen soldier. The guy no leader liked, the guy everyone said was a bad soldier, was currently braving a hail of gunfire to save a man he didn't even know. The ANA soldier had been thrown an incredible distance from the road and was lying helplessly in the open field. His only hope was Wilson, the slowest Mine Hound operator I had ever seen in my entire life. It seemed to take him two whole eternities to reach the fallen man. Once there, he ever so carefully slung the Mine Hound on his back and ripped a tourniquet out of his shoulder pocket. He then went to work on what was left of the man's leg.

As the enemy took note of a lone American soldier in an open field, their attention quickly turned towards the easy target. Watching all this transpire, Doc Gio and Douglas busted out from the safety of the mud hut and aggressively moved towards Wilson's location. Like the good paratroopers they were, the two men used buddy-team movements to cross the field. They took turns running short distances while covering each other with fire from their M4s. Both men did this knowing full well that they were crossing unchecked IED-ridden terrain. Seeing the two men bound across no man's land led Third Squad to turn and cover their movement with every weapon system they had at their disposal. With the much-needed suppressive fire in place, all the two men had to do now was worry about IEDs.

Exhausted from 100 meters' worth of buddy-team movements, Doc Gio flopped down next to Wilson, where he promptly took over care of the casualty. As he did, Douglas got on the radio and made contact with two Kiowas and an Apache gunship that had just arrived on station. American air power in Afghanistan is an enormous advantage that we don't often truly appreciate after the fact. Just their presence on the battlefield is a relief for all friendlies involved. Our requests for air power are often denied and authorization to fire is almost never given. That said, when we get what we ask for, we are never disappointed!

"Dragon 3–4, this is Charlie 2–9. Do you have eyes on any targets?" Douglas asked the gunships as they circled safely above the action below.

"Roger that, 2–9, we have two combatants at your 2 o'clock," a female voice replied from the gunship.

"Stand by for authorization to engage," Douglas told the birds as they eagerly awaited the go-ahead to fire.

After Doc finished applying tourniquets and other necessary aid to the downed ANA soldier, the team prepared to move him to safety. With bullets still cracking and zipping all around them, Doc Gio and Wilson

16. The Complexities of My Emotions

hoisted the injured man up into a manageable position. As Wilson struggled to lift the man from the ground, he could see rocket-propelled grenades coming at him from all directions. His eyes locked onto one of the smoke streamers left by a projectile and he traced it back to the shooter. Following the smoke trail, he realized that they were coming from the mud hut that Third Squad had taken control of earlier. Come to find out, this was the Afghan Army's attempt at suppressive fire. Not knowing where the enemy was, they were blanketing the area with RPGs in all directions. One of the wayward projectiles zipped right over Wilson's head. Just as he realized that the RPGs were at least intended to be helpful, Douglas got authorization to fire, and he cleared the birds to go hot immediately.

From the ECP, I could see the birds circle around and get into an attack formation. Their target was a large mud hut filled with enemy personnel, including the sniper. The Apache was the first to fire, and it chose to start the party with Hellfire missiles. At just under 1,000 miles an hour, the missiles appeared to almost instantaneously reach their target. Upon impact, they completely engulfed the enemy position in smoke, moon dust and debris. I was not disappointed.

With a backdrop of flying debris and the echoes of gunfire in their ears, Wilson and Doc ran as fast as they could back to Third Squad's location. They attempted to use the path that Wilson had swept on his way to the injured man, but it was near impossible. The path was unmarked and they could only approximate it at best. Douglas followed behind the two men, taking a second to bask in a job well done.

Once back in the mud hut, Doc Gio and Wilson set the injured man down and the PL started a Nine Line MedEvac for him. At that time, Douglas climbed up on the roof to assess the target that the Apache had just engaged. Two direct hits from the Hellfire missiles did a great deal to discourage the enemy in the area. Just in case the Hellfire missiles were not convincing enough, Douglas authorized the Kiowas to take turns strafing the enemy position with their .50 caliber machine guns. As the smoke cleared and the debris settled, the gunfire began to wane. Now there were just random cracks and whizzes from both sides as the surviving enemy personnel in the area made their escape. From the safety of the sky, one of the Kiowas could see at least two dead enemy fighters in the structure that they had hit. They could also see several unarmed men fleeing to the west. Their last strafing run with the .50 cal must have been all the convincing they needed. Rules of engagement dictate that unarmed enemy personnel can't be engaged, and the bad guys are well aware of this. They are known for taking advantage of the fact that they can throw down their weapons and run away without fear of being shot in the back. This rule was a luxury they did not afford us.

As the gunships were forced to leave due to low fuel, the sound of their rotors was replaced by those of the all-too-familiar MedEvac helicopter. By this time in the deployment, we had done so many MedEvacs I could tell the difference between the types of birds by sound alone. So one could imagine my preoccupation as I came to the grim realization that Third Squad was MedEvac'ing someone from their element. Lemmon and I both went to the edge of the ECP, as if this would somehow allow us to see who was injured. Instead all we saw was the sputter of a yellow smoke and the propeller wash of a UH-60 pummeling four men carrying a stretcher. We stood and watched the handoff in an attempt, at the very least, to see what kind of uniform the man on the stretcher was wearing. Unfortunately, from our position we were only allotted glimpses of green figures through the yellow smoke and moon dust.

"Everyone is just one colored smoke away from home," Lemmon said as we watched the tail rotors of the MedEvac bird pull the final puffs of yellow smoke off into the distance.

After what seemed like a week of waiting, Third Squad started to trickle their way back to the ECP. Now was the moment of truth, when Lemmon and I could finally see who it was that the yellow smoke had called home. Wilson was the first to leave and the first to return. He waltzed into the ECP with the same goofy smile that he had left with. He waved as he came in and headed straight for the tents. He was acting as if it had been just another patrol, and I had no idea that he had in reality been the hero of the day.

"Wilson, you have to clear your weapon before you go back to the tents, dammit!" Sanders yelled as he shook his head.

"Sanders, who got hit with what?" I asked impatiently as he was checking Wilson's M4, ensuring that it was indeed clear.

"Oh, just some ANA guy who wouldn't stay on the path," he said, lackadaisically making his way back to the tents.

As the rest of the element made their way into the ECP, I thought about how little we actually worry about the well-being of the ANA. It may be bad to say it, but it was always a relief to hear that it was the ANA that took the hit instead of one of us. Maybe that's just how you compartmentalize it. Maybe it's just the way you rationalize the fact that someone has to get hurt. You're not allowed to do this job and have everyone come home safe and sound; that's just not how it works. Thus, you create some kind of mental hierarchy of who you would rather get hurt if you had to

16. The Complexities of My Emotions

choose. Every day you get through when it is one of them and not one of us puts you one step closer to getting home in one piece, I suppose.

A few weeks after Wilson and the guys got back, they actually put Wilson in for a medal. His squad leader wanted to give him an Army Commendation with Valor Device for bravery in the face of danger. That ANA soldier survived solely because of his actions. Had he not acted as quickly as he did, the man would have no doubt bled to death. The request was, of course, promptly denied. First Sergeant decided that Wilson was just doing his job and that he by no means went above and beyond the call of duty. Most of us felt that it had more to do with the fact that he didn't want to give an ARCOM with V device to some turd private who couldn't stay out of trouble. They denied Doc Gio's attempt to get a Combat Action Badge (CAB) from the operation as well. For some reason, First Sergeant did not want to give him a CAB since he had already received his Combat Medic Badge earlier in the deployment. This again is a bit odd, because the battalion had no problem giving a Combat Action Badge to first lieutenants who heard gunfire off in the distance, even when all they did was cower in the grass and hope for the best. Rank definitely has a lot to do with what awards and medals a soldier receives.

– 17 –

To Check or Not to Check

In the final days of July, we were tasked with expanding our company's AO. Due to the size of the operation, we would need to work alongside Third Platoon. The mission dictated that Third Platoon would clear two small village sets to the southeast of COP Nalgham. As they cleared through, our platoon would take up the rear of the element and clear the existing road of IEDs, so it could be expanded. Third Platoon would not be using the road to enter the village because it was the most likely avenue of approach and thus the most dangerous. Once the road was expanded, we would then build two checkpoints that would be manned by U.S. personnel for the remainder of the deployment. The mission was to take around two weeks in total from the beginning of tactical operations to the completion of the second checkpoint.

The mission began at 0600 on a clear, hot summer day in Afghanistan. Third Platoon headed out to clear the villages ahead of us just as planned. While we were waiting to mount up and conduct our clearing operation, we could hear Third Platoon exchanging fire with the Talibros in the area. They were only a little over a mile from our location at COP Nalgham. This, however, was expected: our platoon had pushed into the village a few weeks earlier in the deployment, and we were met with heavy resistance consisting of a complex ambush complete with IED and enemy sniper. Despite our past exploits in the area, reports over the radio gave us the impression that Third Platoon was well in control of the engagement. They had sustained no casualties and they were pushing the enemy out as expected.

Since the battle was well within the capabilities of Third Platoon, we headed out as planned at 0900 in a large convoy of MATVs, MaxxPros, front-end loaders and the LMTV. A short 200 meters outside of COP Nal-

17. To Check or Not to Check

gham, our leaders decided it was best to exit the trucks and start the slow, methodical push forward. On site, Walker and I dismounted to take the first shift sweeping the road. Walker was a younger guy with a Southern drawl straight from an old western movie. He was around my height and build and had the classic cancer-patient Army haircut that we all sported. He had literally finished basic training two weeks prior to deployment. He was as low on the totem pole as one could possibly be, so he was oftentimes given the worst tasks in the platoon. Despite his status within the platoon, he had a positive demeanor and was as about as American as one could be. He did everything for love of God and country. He eventually grew into a great soldier and is perhaps the most reliable person I have ever met. Once he had prepped the Mine Hound, I told him that we would clear the road in sections up one side and back down the other. With an affirmative nod, he turned toward the road and began sweeping.

I followed closely behind Walker, scanning the area for threats while listening to the firefight that still raged in the distance. Every once in a while, a few stray rounds would zip over our heads toward an undetermined destination. We were pretty accustomed to this by now and Walker didn't even seem to notice them. He just swept, intently listening to the sounds his sweeper made as he worked it side to side. Around 100 meters from the trucks, Walker had a huge hit on the Mine Hound. The ground-penetrating radar and the metal detector both maxed out at the same time, ringing out with the unit's distinctive gobbling sound.

"Hooah," Walker said as he gave the hand-and-arm signal for halt.

"That's definitely something," I said as I looked over his shoulder just in time to see the Mine Hound hit twelve out of fourteen on the indicator.

"Ya think we should call it up or should I just step on it for verification?" he asked with a straight face.

"Step on it? Do you think it is something other than an IED?" I asked, confused.

"Well, I'm about as sure that it is an IED as a guy could be," he said, somewhat nervous now.

"Well, get back. I'll call it up, man!" I said, even more confused than before.

"I can't handle being yelled at by the PSG one more time, dude. I would rather risk it," he said, noticeably torn by the decision.

"Fuck that! He can yell at me, man. You don't even need to talk to him," I said as I grabbed the hand mic on my radio.

"I don't know, man. I could be wrong," Walker said, as I broke the radio chatter.

"Break, break, break. This is Charlie 2–1 Bravo, we need EOD for suspected IED, over," I said into the mic.

"Roger that. They are en route. Move back, over," replied the PL from the other side of the radio.

After the PL gave us the go-ahead to move back, I had Walker mark the IED's location and we got the hell up out of that bitch. Leaving a giant chalk X-marks-the-spot, we turned toward the trucks. As we headed back, I took the lead, and Walker slung his Mine Hound and picked up his rifle to help me scan. We stayed vigilant, but all the rounds that we could hear flying over were fairly far above our heads. It was unlikely that we would be hit by any strays as there were buildings in between us and the engagement.

As we approached the first vehicle in the convoy, I could see the EOD team headed our way. I told Walker to jump in the back of our MaxxPro and that I would stay behind to explain the situation to EOD. Staff Sergeant King was pretty surprised when I told him that Walker had hit a twelve with the Mine Hound. He was certain that there had to be something buried there, given the size of the reading. I then showed him how Walker had marked the spot; we could see the giant X from where we were standing. Satisfied he had all the information they needed, he motioned for his guys to send out the bomb disposal robot. Since my services were no longer needed, I headed to the MaxxPro that Walker was in to escape the heat. As I was signaling for the driver to drop the ramp, the PSG came around from the other side of the truck.

"You guys are slowing us down, Sonnerson. Those EOD guys better find something. The Army keeps rolling along, Roger," he grumbled as he passed by me to check on Staff Sergeant King.

"Alrighty," I mumbled, still waving at the driver to drop the ramp.

Once the driver finally woke up and saw me waving, he dropped the ramp for me. I then walked the short distance around back to the only air-conditioned truck we had. Once inside, I sat down to find Walker staring at me in anticipation. He was waiting for me to tell him how pissed-off the PSG was that he had halted the operation. Much to his surprise, I reported that he was in a much better mood than usual. As Walker breathed a sigh of relief, the voice of Staff Sergeant King came over the radio. He confirmed that he had a positive ID on the IED and that he needed his guys to prep the suit.

While Walker and I were discussing how ridiculous it would have been if he'd have stepped on the IED to check it out, the passenger door of the MaxxPro swung open. Staff Sergeant Hunter was sitting in the passenger seat and the PL was there to give him an update on the situation. The PL explained that King had found a massive IED that was more than big enough to take out a MaxxPro. He says it looks like a five-gallon jug attached to a 115 shell. As I heard this, Walker and I slowly turned toward each other and burst out laughing.

"Well, I would not have felt a thing," Walker laughed.

"We would have both been pink-misted. No, we would have just ceased to exist like we had been teleported to another dimension," I said, still laughing.

As we continued to imagine just how awesome this could have been, the PL explained to Staff Sergeant Hunter that King was going to BIP the IED. After he finished up, Walker and I would need to jump out and continue onward.

Just a few short minutes later, the radio cracked with, "One minute till BIP."

"I can't wait to see how big this fucking BIP is," Blackman said from the driver seat. He was holding his phone up and recording. Through his phone I could see Staff Sergeant King and the PSG as they took cover behind the vehicle in front of us.

Once behind the truck, Staff Sergeant King gave a three-two-one count and pulled the plunger to set off the controlled detonation. With a roar and a huge cloud of dust, the IED sent debris up over 100 meters into the air. Given the moon dust that covered the road, we could watch the shock wave travel from the IED to the trucks and beyond. Once the shock wave passed us by, the trucks were littered with small pieces of debris that harmlessly rained down around us.

Blast in place of an IED found by Walker (courtesy Norman Blackman).

"That was a lot bigger than I thought it would be," Blackman said, noticeably surprised.

"Oh, yeah?" Staff Sergeant Hunter replied.

"That was found by Johnny Wayne Walker. Walker, show me your face," Blackman said as he turned the camera to the back of the truck to get Walker in the shot.

Walker just sat up straight and smiled as the camera panned his way.

Now that the BIP was complete, I knew that Walker and I had to go out there and pick up where we had left off. When I lowered the ramp on our vehicle, I was met with an oppressive heat. It almost seemed like it was trying to keep me from exiting as it mixed with the cool air from the AC. As I jumped down from the MaxxPro, I saw three brand-new MATVs pulling up to the rear of our convoy. Judging by the look of the vehicles, it could only be someone of some importance, or perceived importance, anyway. Battalion commanders (BC) and above have trucks that work like they are supposed to, with functioning doors and air-conditioning. I have even seen some of them that had mini fridges with cold drinks in the back. Believe it or not, the battalion commander didn't feel like climbing over his driver's lap to exit the vehicle. As Walker jumped out of the truck beside me, he locked onto what I was staring at. Walker was more in the know than I was because he knew why the vehicles had arrived. Apparently, the BC had decided to bring some POGs (people other than grunts) down during the operation to get their CABs. Walker powered up his Mine Hound while I waited to see if any war heroes jumped out of the MATVs. By this time in the day, all the real shooting had stopped, so I wasn't sure if they would be able to get any fake CABs or not. Walker and I left the fancy trucks in place for someone else to worry about and headed out to continue the clearing operation.

Over the next few hours, Walker and I cleared the entirety of the road and the area for the prospective checkpoint. Once we gave the all-clear, the convoy circled the wagons, and everyone started to unload the Hesco walls and fenceposts that would soon take the shape of a checkpoint. It took no time at all for us to align the first two walls of the outpost so that the front-end loaders could start filling them in.

* * *

Walker, Staff Sergeant Alonzo and I were setting up the Hesco walls with the help of a first lieutenant by the name of Tillers. He was one of the war heroes who had been dropped off by the BC. He was almost as big as an eighth-grade schoolgirl and he carried himself like he was scared

17. To Check or Not to Check 153

of his own shadow. He did prove to be a hard worker and seemed eager to prove himself to the big tough infantry guys. It wasn't that I disliked him; he was just extremely out of place, and it was somewhat annoying to watch him struggle to fit in. It was clear he was an office POG who had come by for glory, fabricated or real.

As Staff Sergeant Alonzo and I were setting up a Hesco wall, a stray burst of automatic fire whizzed overhead. Staff Sergeant Alonzo paid it no mind as he finished extending the Hesco wall. I, on the other hand, took a short pause and looked up from what I was doing to check it out. Staff Sergeant Alonzo was clearly annoyed with me. He was trying to get this checkpoint done and I was slowing us down.

"Those aren't anywhere near us," Staff Sergeant Alonzo stated as he saw me looking up from what I was doing.

"Roger, just checking it out, Sergeant," I replied.

As Staff Sergeant Alonzo and I completed the wall, we saw the PSG running frantically from truck to truck, pushing everyone out of his way as he went.

"Take cover, Roger. Don't just stand out in the open, dammit!" the PSG screamed as more rounds flew over.

Staff Sergeant Alonzo just shrugged his shoulders and motioned for me to move toward the nearest point of cover. While we were casually walking to the corner of the Hesco wall, we passed by Lieutenant Tillers, who had glued himself to the ground. He was spread-eagled in the open field with giant fistfuls of grass in each hand. He was desperately using the shrubbery to pull himself as close to the earth as humanly possible. It looked as if he was attempting to pull himself into the ground! Staff Sergeant Alonzo looked at Lieutenant Tillers, then at me, almost as if to get confirmation on what this guy was doing.

Once we got to the corner, we stood there waiting for Third Platoon to achieve suppressive fire. It took just over a minute for all fire to come to a halt, and not one round flew even remotely near our actual location. Staff Sergeant Alonzo looked almost annoyed by the fact that we had to stop working and stand there waiting in the scorching heat.

"What the fuck is this guy doin', ya'll?" Walker said, dragging his words.

Turning to see what Walker was pointing at, I saw Lieutenant Tillers still aggressively pulling himself toward the ground. Both hands were clinging to those mounds of grass he had been using earlier.

"Just leave him be and get back to work," Staff Sergeant Alonzo said, realizing that guys were about to start ridiculing an officer.

It doesn't matter how pathetic or screwed-up an officer is, it is never OK for a bunch of privates to make fun of him. This is as far as the Army is concerned, of course.

While Walker and I were pulling the next Hesco wall toward the checkpoint, Lieutenant Tillers was behind us, slowly composing himself. He stood up, took several deep breaths, and started pumping his fists toward the ground while telling himself encouraging words.

"You got this. You got this. You're a soldier," he said to himself in a reassuring tone.

"Are you trying to fuck my mom right now?" I said in disbelief.

"I know, right? Is this guy serious?" Walker said, standing up the wall.

Once composed and reassured, Lieutenant Tillers came over to us to talk about his first firefight.

"Not bad for my first contact, huh? Is this what you guys feel like every day? I feel like I could get a few rounds off next go around," Lieutenant Tillers said as some dirt and grass fell from his helmet.

"Let's hope not," I said, imagining him accidentally shooting me in the back with his eyes closed.

I could tell by the look on Walker's face that he was as terrified by the thought as I was. We both knew if he started shooting, he would be more likely to hit one of us than any bad guys, especially considering that they were nowhere near our location. Despite our concerns, Tillers was quite proud of himself. He couldn't seem to stop pacing back and forth, telling himself and anyone who would listen how awesome he was, leaving Walker and me to build the next section of the outpost by ourselves. It was funny at first, but after a while, it was just ridiculous and sad.

Needless to say, when I got back to the States, I saw Lieutenant Tillers marching around the halls of battalion headquarters wearing his CAB. He was telling his crazy war stories from that day in Afghanistan. As one would imagine, he left out a few key details while perhaps adding some others. But, hey, some things you check and others you don't.

– 18 –

Ice Cream and Lattes

We spent the last few weeks of August packing away our gear, cleaning weapons, and preparing to return home. After we wrapped up everything at Nalgham, we headed back to Kandahar Airfield, or KAF. There, all we would have to do was wait for a flight home. KAF is a giant base full of non-combat personnel, or what we call POGs. The POGs who live and work there are, for the most part, support personnel like cooks and paralegals. I am not saying that they are not important, because they are. It's just important to note that they do not live a soldier's life like infantrymen or grunts do. They do not go on patrol, fire their weapons, or participate in what one would typically imagine a soldier doing. They stay on the base and live a life on deployment that is unbelievably comfortable. KAF has a soccer field, bowling alley, pizzeria, weekly salsa nights, and most importantly of all, showers. I had not even seen a real shower in months, so I was taking full advantage of the fact that there was one right outside of my tent. I was in there twice a day in an attempt to get seven months of smell off me.

We spent a week at KAF just scoffing at the POGs and the crazy shit that they were doing. Our disgust for their activities was half due to jealousy, half out of amazement. I once watched a POG drop her rifle on the ground while she was fumbling with an ice cream cone and drinking a triple latte. When the rifle hit the ground, the magazine fell out and slid across the ground. While she was bending down to pick up the magazine, an entire scoop of vanilla ice cream fell into the mag well. While the sprinkles were still bouncing on the ground, she crammed the magazine in on top of the ice cream.

When Blackman saw this, he yelled at her and said, "Hey, don't you think you might want to clean that thing out first?"

She just scoffed at him and said, "What! It's not like we even use them!" Then she stormed off like he was the one who was fucked up.

This is just one example of the crazy things that people on these huge bases would do. The majority of the Army has so little to do with combat that it never even crosses their minds.

All the hilarious POG antics aside, the week in KAF was quite pleasant and we enjoyed all the POG amenities more than they did. Every night, Blackman, Lemmon, and I would sit in the middle of a boardwalk between the beach volleyball court and the soccer field. We could be found there, smoking cigars and listening to the "Simple Man" remake by Shinedown on repeat. We would sit and enjoy the night air saying almost nothing. These few nights are still some of the most peaceful I have had in my entire life. I had nowhere to be and nothing to worry about; all I had to do was wait for a ride home.

* * *

When we finally got our ride home, we were super pumped, and we all got on the plane as ready as we could possibly be. I sat down next to a female major and fastened my seat belt, smiling from ear to ear.

"Why are you smiling?" she asked, noticeably frustrated by my uncontainable joy.

"Oh, I am just super excited to go home, ma'am," I said.

"Why? It's just the same job for less pay back in the States," she scoffed.

"Hmm," I thought, "Well, you must be a POG because my job is very different stateside." I, of course, just said, "Either way, I am very excited, ma'am."

"What's that on your body armor?" she asked with a look of disgust on her face.

"Where, ma'am?" I said, looking down at my kit.

"Is that blood on your body armor?" she asked.

I looked down and saw a tiny little spot of blood on my kit left over from putting a tourniquet on an ANA dude who'd stepped on an IED.

She looked me straight in the face and asked, "How in the hell did you get blood on your body armor, soldier?"

As I started to explain myself, she yelled for the Airman in charge of the bird. She then demanded that I be moved to the back of the plane away from everyone else, because I was too disgusting to sit by. Being a low-ranking piece of shit, I had no say in the matter and just did as I was told. That's the Army for you, always standing on ceremony.

Once away from the major, it did not take me too long to regain my

18. Ice Cream and Lattes

high spirits. I was going to go home, buy a $1,000 Italian suit, drink all the booze in the state of North Carolina, and pretend like I wasn't even in the Army. Thus, these POGs could have their fun for now, but in the end, I was going to win this fucking game. All I had to do was endure a few more days of the Army's nonsense. Then I would get to spend my first day out from underneath its goddamn thumb in over seven months, and no stupid POG was going to ruin that for me. Especially one who couldn't even fathom how a soldier might get blood on his body armor while on deployment to Afghanistan with the United States Army.

– 19 –

But Nobody Died, Right?

More than a week after POGapalooza in KAF, we finally landed on United States soil. All I wanted to do was get away from those in charge of me for a few days and relax. There was, however, one thing standing in my way, the stupid welcome-home ceremony. It was supposed to be a welcome-home party for us, the soldiers returning from Afghanistan. In reality, however, it was a parade put on for the families and those much higher in rank than me. This particular ceremony would have us march from the plane into the hangar, where all the soldiers' families awaited us. Once inside, we would march in place singing Army songs and yell out things like the Soldier's Creed. Once we'd finished our part, we would then be required to stand perfectly still at attention while we listened to a never-ending slew of speeches from officers whom I had never met. While all this went on, we would be wanting desperately to be released to see our families or in my case get away from the Army. If they really wanted to welcome me home properly, it would not include having us marching around, singing songs, and listening to speeches. The only thing that the Army brass loves more than making the peons march around is forcing them to stand around and listen to speeches. This was what I hated the most about the Army, drill, and ceremony. Nothing made less sense to me than us having to put on a show for our own homecoming ceremony. Nevertheless, I would be forced to endure it.

After the ceremony finally came to an end, we were released to go get our duffle bags from a flatbed truck out in front of the hangar. Everyone sprinted to the truck to get their shit and get the hell out of there.

While we were unloading the bags, some of the stupider NCOs started yelling and making threats. They wanted to go home right now and if we didn't get those bags unloaded right then they were going to fuck us up.

19. But Nobody Died, Right?

"Really," I thought, "you're going to smoke us now that we are home, done, and in front of people's wives and kids? I won't do a single push-up. Not today, motherfucker." One of the particularly stupid NCOs jumped up into the back of the truck with the duffle bags so everyone could see him. He'd had enough of our lackadaisical attitude and decided that we needed to do some remedial PT. Most people got into the push-up position, but I just stood off to the side by some officers. There was no way I was going to do a single pushup! As everyone was banging out reps, the NCO stood in the back of the truck ranting about time management and moving with a sense of purpose. I'm not a rocket scientist, but to me it seemed like it may actually take us longer to get done if we wasted time doing pushups. As I was standing there fuming, I looked over beside the truck where I saw DC talking and laughing with his family. "Not a care in the world," I thought as he threw his head back and laughed at something his dad said. That was DC for you, just doing his own thing. After the NCO felt like he had made his point, he let everyone stop and go back to work on the bags.

Everyone jumped up, moving even slower now, since they were all super pissed off and a little tired. After we finally got done with all the fuck-fuck games, we headed back to our new barracks rooms. "Finally, peace," I thought as I threw my bags down in my new room. I had purposefully asked my family not to come visit till the following weekend, since I knew the homecoming was going to be super stupid. The evening had validated my choice perfectly. Even I had not expected it to be as dumb as it was.

* * *

At 0200 I lay down on a real bed, ready to sleep the best night of sleep in my entire life. I lay there for about an hour staring at the ceiling, trying to decide what I was going to do with my new-found freedom at home. I soon realized that I would not be sleeping, so I decided to head to Walmart to buy the items I needed for my empty barracks room. Not having a car, I called a cab to take me to Wally World.

As I waited out front, two of the medics from other platoons came out and started to jump in their car. Just as they were about to leave, they asked me where I was headed. As luck would have it, they too were going to Walmart, and they would be glad to give me a ride.

Our trip to Walmart was uneventful but weirdly peaceful. I had not performed a regular human person task in normal clothes for seven months and it was just short of a Zen-like experience for me. It was weird not to be desperately exhausted with ten things to do twenty minutes ago.

Once back at the barracks, I spent the rest of the morning organizing my room and waiting for someone to be awake. Since most of the guys in my unit were hanging out with their families, I started calling some of my old Special Forces Qualification Course buddies. Around 0700 I got ahold of Lee and the soon-to-be-legendary Magnum, and we decided to grab breakfast at a local diner. I had yet to sleep, but was not in the slightest bit tired, and could not wait to see my good old buddies from the Q course.

Upon meeting at the diner, we exchanged pleasantries and began talking about what everyone had been doing for the last several months.

Out of the blue, Lee asked, "So, are you a real infantryman now?"

"What do you mean?" I asked, cramming half a pancake in my mouth.

"You guys didn't actually see any combat, did you?" he asked.

"Some, but nothing crazy," I said.

"What, like some mortars hitting across the other side of your FOB?" he asked.

"No, we got into a few little firefights and hit a some IEDs," I said.

"But *you* didn't, right?" he said more as a statement than a question.

"No, I fired some rounds, why?" I asked.

"Well, I just can't see how you could do OK in a gunfight, that's all," he said in a superior tone.

Starting to get super pissed-off, I said, "Well, I hate to disappoint you, but I fired bullets, grenades, did first aid, and the whole shebang."

"But nobody died, right?" he stated.

"I am afraid motherfuckers did die!" I said, nearly at a yell.

"But you didn't see your best friend die right in front of your eyes, though, right?" he said.

"You sure hold me to some high standards for someone who has never fucking deployed!" I yelled.

"I am just trying to see if you guys actually did anything, that's all. Jesus! Calm down!" he said, offended.

"Well, fuck me! Sorry, I am the one who's an asshole here?" I said.

And with that, we sat in silence for a few minutes and then changed the subject.

The problem with deploying is that when you come back, everyone either thinks you are a huge liar or that you are some kind of ninja assassin. There is no middle ground. Being in the infantry, at least for me, is a lot like blue collar work. Everyone just gets in there and grinds it out doing a lot a manual labor, and occasionally, you shoot some rounds. Even when you are shooting, it's still a lot like a factory job. Each person does his little piece of the job and things just plug along slowly and methodically.

Every once in a while, something violent and unexpected happens, like an IED. That said, one's ability to go back to the factory-work mentality and put the assembly line back to work defines his effectiveness. If one runs around freaking out, he is not overly effective. But if he calls the medic, reports to higher command, and ensures people are pulling security, things start to go his way. Keep everyone on the line doing his little job and things go well, just like in a factory. It's not sexy, it won't get you any free beers, but that's how it is, or at least how it was for me.

– 20 –

Night on the Big Town

It was finally our first real day off since the beginning of the deployment. Not only that, it was the night we had all been waiting for, we were going to put suits on our bodies and booze in our bellies. We had talked about this night for weeks now and all the pieces were in place. We had our Italian suits tailored, and we were going to go to Raleigh to have some sushi and hit the clubs. The next day we were going to get up run a 5K in children's superhero costumes, and then hit the town again that night.

We busted into the first club wearing our suits and our terrible Army haircuts like we owned the place. Blackman was in the lead, wearing his all-white suit with an unlit cigar in one hand and the most pretentious hand gesture I have ever seen in the other. Thompson swaggered in behind him with his top hat, suspenders, and black and white wingtip shoes. Chapman, Rodriguez, Odinson, Townsend, and myself were close behind. All of us were laughing at just how much of an asshole Blackman was. Lemmon, as always, was pulling up the rear at a pace that would almost challenge a ninety-year-old tortoise. Once at the bar, we started the night with two shots of tequila apiece.

As we finished the shots, one of the hostesses came up to Blackman and asked, "Do you guys want to purchase a VIP room for two hundred dollars an hour?"

"No, we won't be staying long," he scoffed as he waved her away with the unlit cigar.

"Oh, you don't like our club?" she asked.

"Oh, it's OK, I guess," Blackman replied.

"I can see if I can get you guys a deal if you will stay," she said politely.

"Come back to me with the deal and we will see," Blackman said with another pretentious wave of the hand.

"Wow, you're an asshole," Chapman said, laughing.

"What?" said Blackman with a genuine look of confusion.

We got a few more drinks and went out on the balcony to smoke some cigars. Just as we were lighting them up, the same hostess came out onto the balcony. She was able to convince the owner to give us fine gentlemen the biggest VIP room all night for free. Everyone in the group was quite impressed by this, other than Blackman, of course. He made it clear that he couldn't promise we would stay, but that he would at least check out the room. With a glimmer of hope in her eyes, she ran off to prepare the room for our arrival. They must have really thought we had some serious money to spend if they were willing to give us free VIP service. Blackman might have been an asshole, but it was hard for me to argue with his results.

After finishing our cigars, we all went and sat down in the VIP area, quite impressed by Blackman's ability to get us not only a free room, but also a free bottle of champagne. With the room came women. Just because we looked like we had a little money, everyone wanted to be our friends. It is really quite ridiculous how well you can get treated if you wear a nice suit and sit in a room that is restricted to others. As we were sitting there, the waitress brought a group of girls over to our little VIP area and asked us if we wanted them to sit down. Blackman looked them up and down and nodded with just a hint of superiority. The girls all sat down with us and we started to mingle.

"What are you guys celebrating?" one of the girls asked.

"Not dying," responded Chapman.

"I'm sorry?" the girl said, a little confused.

"We just got back from deployment," Chapman said as he poured her a glass of champagne.

"Oh, you guys are in the military or something?" she asked, a bit skeptical.

"Yep, the Army to be exact," Chapman said, handing out another glass of champagne.

"No, you're not. Army guys don't make shit for money," said another girl skeptically.

"You're right. We just get these terrible haircuts because we think it is funny to walk around looking like cancer patients," Chapman admitted.

"I knew it," she said, with a satisfied look on her face.

Chapman and I exchanged confused looks while the first girl asked, "Well, what do you guys do, then?"

"We run a multimillion-dollar agriculture center in Ohio," Thompson stated in a very matter-of-fact way.

"That's what I thought," said the first girl, quite proud of herself.

"You thought that we ran a multimillion-dollar ag-business?" I asked, noticeably frustrated.

"Well, no, but I knew you weren't in the Army, that's for sure," she stated.

"You got us," Lemmon interjected as he raised his glass for a toast. "Here's to never being in the Army again," he said with a nod to the girls.

With that, we did all that we could to die by way of alcohol poisoning.

* * *

The next few hours were a blur, but I do remember stumbling out of the club looking for Lemmon and Chapman. I was so drunk that I could just barely walk. I stopped at the edge of the street and tried to scan the area for any sign of the others. While searching the entrances of nearby clubs and bars, I was having a great deal of trouble stabilizing myself. So I posted up against a trash can facing the street to continue my scan for the guys. I made sure to prop myself up in the most presentable manner possible, just in case any ladies wanted to talk to a drunk idiot in a three-piece suit. As I was marveling at how sober I had made myself appear, a well-dressed man and woman got out of their car and headed straight for me.

"Put her in a good spot," the man said as he handed me his keys and hurried past me to the club.

"What is he talking about? Does he think I am going to park his fucking car?" I asked myself.

"Oh, here he is, honey," said a lady to my left. "You're the valet, right?" she said, as her husband handed me another set of car keys.

"Oh, holy shit," I thought. "I am standing in the valet area of this club, in a suit with no jacket on, and everyone thinks I am the valet."

"Where the fuck is my jacket?" I asked myself out loud as I looked around on the ground, like it might actually be there. While I was figuring all this out, I was handed three more sets of keys. What am I going to do with five sets of keys?" I thought. Just as I was deciding whether or not to risk a DUI and grand theft auto in order to park these vehicles in the funniest places ever, Chapman yelled my name from across the street. Directly across the way, there stood Chapman and Lemmon. They had been right in front of me the whole time. The two men were waiting in line to go into some underground club.

I looked at the keys and then back at Chapman, trying to decide what

20. Night on the Big Town

to do. I then pushed off the trash can, flipped open the door on it, and threw all five sets in the trash. I stumbled my way across the street, nearly getting hit by a car. I approached my friends just in time for the bouncer of the club to tell everyone outside to wait there. As he disappeared into the club, Chapman and Lemmon ushered me to the front of the line with them.

"What the hell were you doing over there, man?" Lemmon asked me.

"Just parking some cars, bro," I said.

As I was confusing Lemmon, some girls skipped ahead to the front of the line and handed Chapman their IDs. Without missing a beat, he flipped them over a few times and handed them back. Then said, "You're in," and in they went.

"Oh, I have got to do this," I thought. I stepped up next to him and we both started checking IDs and letting people into the club. I was so drunk I couldn't even figure out what states these IDs were from, but it didn't matter. I just kept flipping them over and saying, "You're in!"

After we had gotten the hang of our new profession, the real bouncers all came bursting out of the door. They were pissed that a bunch of drunk morons had been letting people into the club. As one of them demanded an explanation, the other reached for Lemmon's shoulder. Smiling from ear to ear Lemmon bolted. Not wanting to get left behind, Chapman was hot on his heels. As the two men broke into a full stride, I threw the ID I had in my hand straight up in the air and ran like hell. The three of us were laughing like a bunch of schoolgirls all the way down the street.

I stopped a few blocks down from the underground club to catch my breath and realized that I had lost both Chapman and Lemmon once again. After a few choice words, I composed myself and began searching for the two of them. "Well, they can't have gone far," I thought. I started poking my head into little side bars and restaurants looking for the two of them. As I did, I interrogated doormen and bouncers as to their whereabouts. I figured that two drunk guys in suits should be pretty easy to spot in this part of town. They had to be causing havoc wherever they were, so people would probably remember them if they saw them.

After a few short minutes of searching, I gave up. I decided to just go into a bar sit down, have a drink and see what happened. I picked a small hole-in-the-wall place, sat by the entrance, and ordered a beer and a shot of tequila. I pounded the shot, and while I was sipping on the beer, a lady in her mid-forties, still quite attractive, caught my eye. She got up from her stool at the end of the bar and headed straight for me. "Oh, my," I thought, "a lady wants to talk to me. Whatever will I do?"

"Hey! You looking for your friends?" she asked as I fixed my tie.

"Maybe," I said smoothly, as if it were some kind of pick-up line.

"You either are or you're not," she said, confused by my answer. "You have been scanning the bar constantly since you sat down. Are you looking for those other guys in suits?" she asked again, noticeably annoyed.

"Oh, yeah, are they here?" I asked.

"They were. I had to throw them out of here for being assholes in my bar," she said.

"Oh, sounds like them. What did they do?" I asked.

"The one with the big head decided to piss all over my stairs and when I yelled at him to get out, he slipped in his own piss and fell down almost the entire flight of stairs," she scowled.

"Definitely them," I thought.

After regaling me with the tale of my long-lost comrades, she pointed me in the direction they had headed when they left her bar. The group of drunks had run across the street toward a bar called the Fourth Floor Club. According to her, they were laughing like a bunch of drunken hyenas the whole way there. I thanked her for her help and made my exit, hoping I was not too far behind them.

I crossed the street to the four-story building and headed for the elevator. I was way too drunk for stairs. When I went to push the up button, I was greeted with a gigantic out of order sign. This, of course, was exactly what I had hoped I would find. I made my way up the stairs slowly, avoiding all the vomit and piss. "Chapman has been here," I thought.

Finally, I reached the Fourth Floor Club and stepped up to pay the doorman. As I was handing him a ten, I scanned the club for Chapman or Lemmon. The club was on the roof with one giant rectangle bar in the middle and waist-high railing all the way around the outer edge of the roof, which formed one large balcony. The view of the capital was actually pretty nice, even if I was seeing double.

As I stepped up to the bar, I saw Blackman and Chapman surrounded by about five girls, and they all seemed to be getting along quite well. I came up to the group next to Chapman to see what they were talking about. Chapman was extremely drunk at this point and his responses to what the girls were saying were ridiculous.

"No, seriously, thank you for your service," one of the girls said.

"You don't know me!" Chapman slurred as if she had insulted him.

"He is so drunk," one of the girls said.

"No, you don't understand. Thank you for your service," she said again.

"Fuck you, bitch!" Chapman said right to her face!

The girls recoiled, appalled by his insane answers. Just when I thought things couldn't get any worse, Chapman vomited all over the floor in front of him, splattering vomit on the girls' feet, all of whom were wearing those lace-up sandal heels.

"To the bathroom, man! To the bathroom!" Lemmon yelled as he came out of nowhere. He tried to usher Chapman to his immediate right, where the bathrooms were less than five feet away.

Chapman instead zigged when he should have zagged, choosing to go all the way around the bar. He was vomiting every few steps as Lemmon was trying to corral him to somewhere he could vomit. Chapman finally composed himself after he made it around the entire circumference of the bar, stopping where the entrance was located. Chapman stopped by the doorman, looked him straight in the face, fixed his tie, said "Good day, sir," and then made his exit. The girls, at this time, were screaming at me and Blackman, demanding new shoes and apologies. I had not done anything wrong, so I did as any gentleman would. I left the club with haste and chased after Chapman and Lemmon once more.

Once on the ground floor, I had lost Chapman and Lemmon again. So I decided to just call it a night and head back to the hotel. I hailed a cab and headed that way, still laughing at Chapman's choice to go left instead of right.

* * *

The cab dropped me off in front of the hotel, and there were Lemmon, Thompson, and Chapman sitting on a bench outside of the entrance. Just when I had decided that they were impossible to find, they showed up out of nowhere. As I sat down on the bench next to Chapman, Lemmon was acting as if he may die of starvation at any moment. Given the hour, the rest of us were pretty certain that we wouldn't find anywhere still open. While we were discussing our options, a pizza delivery man jumped out of his car and headed through the entrance of the hotel.

"Hey, are you guys still open?" Chapman asked.

"Nope, this is my last delivery of the night," the deliveryman replied.

"Fuck!" Lemmon said as he kicked a planter in the lobby.

"Hey, we could just buy those pizzas from him," Chapman said.

"What do you mean?" said Lemmon.

"Hey, Thompson, tell him we will give him like a twenty-dollar tip if he sells us those pizzas," I yelled.

Thompson caught up with him and he sold us the pizzas. We handsomely rewarded him for his kindness and headed to our rooms for the night. As we lay around the room eating the pizzas, I reminded everyone that we still had a 5K to run the next day. We all laughed at the thought and got ready for bed. Lemmon passed out on the floor where he was eating pizza, still fully dressed in a thousand-dollar three-piece suit, alligator shoes, fedora, and all. I, on the other hand, took the time to drunk-fold my suit pants and hang my vest up. I then promptly passed out in the chair by the door, laughing to myself about how stupid this race was going to be first thing in the morning.

– 21 –

Superheroes with Drinking Problems

My phone alarm went off bright and early at 0700. "Holy shit," I thought to myself. "I'm still super drunk." I struggled out of the chair in the corner with my head throbbing almost to the point of impairing my vision completely. As I headed toward the bathroom, I stepped over the best-dressed blackout drunk man I had ever seen. Lemmon was still in the exact same position he had been when he lay down a few hours earlier. He had not moved a muscle. The fedora was still perfectly seated atop his head and everything.

Once at the bathroom, I tried to open the door, only for it to hit something on the other side. "What the hell?" I thought. So, like any still-drunk person who needed to use the bathroom would do, I repeatedly bashed the door into whatever was obstructing it. On my fifth or sixth attempt at breaching, I heard a faint moan come from inside the bathroom. It sounded like it could have been Blackman. A quick glance around the room revealed that he was the only paratrooper unaccounted for. I called out his name several times but received no answer. Since he didn't respond, I slowly pushed the door in and forced my way inside the bathroom. He was passed out, sitting on his butt with his legs curled under him using the toilet seat as a pillow. Thinking that this was too good of an opportunity to pass up, I headed out of the room to grab a camera. Camera in hand, I decided to wake up everyone else, so they could see Blackman in his finest hour.

I went around the room waking the troops so we could get ready for the race and laugh at Blackman. Chapman, Rodriguez, and Lemmon started moving, but Odinson, Thompson, and Blackman were, for all intents and purposes, dead to the world. We all laughed at Blackman, took pictures of him, and then started to put our child-size superhero costumes on for the race. Since they were designed for eight- to twelve-year-olds, it would be an understatement to say that they were crushing our nuts! Just when we thought we would have to abandon the costumes, I had a brilliant idea. We could all just cut the crotch out of them and wear our running shorts over top. Everyone agreed that this was a great idea, so we all passed around a KA-BAR Lemmon had brought, modifying our costumes. As we were getting dressed, Townsend knocked on the door to see if we were ready to go.

"Hey, my wife said she would drive us to the race since everyone is still probably drunk," Townsend said, laughing.

"Oh, she's a saint, because no one in here should be driving anywhere," Chapman said as he pulled his Iron Man mask on.

"Holy shit! Look at Lemmon," Townsend said, bursting into laughter.

We all turned to see that Lemmon had cut his Wolverine costume in half, so he could wear it like a shirt. The only problem was that he didn't take into consideration it was a child-size costume. When he put it on, it was way too small and looked like a Wolverine tube top on him. We all laughed, pointed, and called him names, then headed out to where Townsend's wife was waiting to drive us to the third annual Teachers for Education fundraiser 5K. Townsend and I got to the car first and turned to see what was taking Batman, Iron Man, and gay Wolverine so long. Chapman kept tripping over Rodriguez's cape, causing them both to continuously fall down. Lemmon had just given up on the whole endeavor, and was sitting down on one of the beach chairs halfway from the hotel room to the car. I ran back to Lemmon and got him moving, and all six of us piled into the five-passenger vehicle.

"To the races!" Chapman yelled as we hit the road, and off we went.

* * *

Our drunken antics at the hotel had caused us to arrive at the race only a few minutes before registration closed. We stood in the back of a line of about 100 people doubting we would be able to get registered in time for the race. We looked pathetic; guys were dry-heaving and taking turns running to the only Porta-John in the area. As we were enduring the wait, one of the officials came running back to where we were in line.

"You guys want to race?" she asked our group of drunks.

"Yeah, do we have time to sign up?" I asked.

"We have five slots left just for you guys," she said with a smile. "Follow

Townsend, Chapman, Lemmon, Summerfield and Rodriguez after the 5K teacher trot (courtesy Clint Lemmon).

me and I'll get you guys signed in." She turned and headed toward the registration table.

We followed her to the front of the line and signed in for the race. Chapman and Lemmon were still so drunk, Townsend and I had to fill out their registration forms for them. They were so incapacitated we literally had them sign their waivers with Xs. After we had all filled out the necessary paperwork, the race official hurried us to the starting line. There was a mere five minutes until the event would begin.

As we headed to the starting line, people kept stopping us and asking where we were from and what were we doing. Some of them even wanted to take pictures with us. It was really quite ridiculous that everyone was super-excited five drunk idiots had shown up to race in superhero costumes. We took a few pictures and made our way to the starting line, where we waited for the race to begin.

As we were waiting, two attractive young ladies came up to Chapman and Lemmon and started asking what was up with the costumes.

"Why did you guys dress up?" one of them asked.

"'Cause I like to drink," said Chapman, fixing his Iron Man mask.

"What is this fucking race about?" Lemmon asked, confused.

"It's to raise money for the teachers in this district so they can provide a better education for the children of the community," one of the girls replied proudly.

"Education?" Chapman scoffed.

"You don't support education?" the girl asked.

"Never have, never will," Chapman said, shaking his head.

"What?" asked one of the girls. "You know we are teachers, right?"

"Classic mistake," said Chapman, shaking his head again. "Classic mistake."

Just then the whistle blew, and we were off. As I started running, I was struggling to breathe through my ridiculous Captain America mask and my legs felt like cement. As I was suffocating, I watched as Lemmon and Townsend took off like madmen to the front of the pack. I, on the other hand, ran at a pace I could keep without dying. Just as I completed the first mile, I caught up with Lemmon. He was passing older runners and facepalming little kids out of his way. One kid, in particular, was trying really hard to get by him, but Lemmon just kept cutting the kid off and pushing him into the grass. As Lemmon and the kid battled it out, I passed them both on the outside and headed for the halfway point. As I approached the turnaround, I could see Superman headed my way. Townsend was moving fast, and it looked like he may even be leading the race. "Holy shit. If he wins this race drunk in a child-sized Superman costume, I am going to lose my shit," I thought. At the turnaround point, the spectators all cheered for Captain America and Wolverine. As we rounded the corner and headed back toward the finish line, some parents got Lemmon to high-five their kids as he passed.

The whole way, everyone was super-excited to cheer us drunk idiots on. Not long after I was on my way back, I saw Chapman dying from the heat and moving at a snail's pace. Up until that point, I felt like I was hurting, but Chapman looked moments from death. As I rounded the last corner and could see the finish line, I heard the race announcer calling out the play-by-play. While the crowd chanted "Superman," Townsend crossed the finish line in first place! I could not believe that Townsend won after a night of power drinking and shenanigans!

I finished a minute later in third and stopped in the grass near the finish line to wait for the rest of the guys. As I was sipping on some water, Lemmon crossed the finish line with a mob of angry kids not far behind. Not ten feet through the tape, Lemmon threw himself on the ground in the middle of the road. He just lay there catching his breath, forcing everyone else to go around him. Chapman and Rodriguez were not far behind, and we all reunited for pictures with all our adoring fans. While we were taking pictures, one of the race officials came up to Townsend to thank us for coming. She said that everyone was so excited to cheer for us that next year they were going to hold a costume contest in our honor! It was pure insanity how big of a scene we caused at this race. We were all extremely hung over now, and the pictures were becoming nothing short of painful. "Nothing like a 5K run to knock that last bit of drunk off you in the morning," I thought.

As I looked around at the guys, Chapman looked like pure death leaning against a water cooler. Lemmon lay motionless in the grass while kids tugged at his arms to get him up for more pictures. Townsend decided that if we didn't leave right then and there, we would all die on the field. So, on that note, we said our goodbyes and headed back to the hotel. The car ride was silent except for the occasional death rattle from the back seat.

Once back at the hotel, we staggered into our room to find Doc Gio giving Odinson an IV. I explained to Doc Gio that Chapman was just moments from death and that he should take a look at him. So, like a good medic, Doc gave Chapman and some of the other guys the last of the IVs while Lemmon and I pounded some water. We all needed to prepare for our next big day of drinking. I didn't really need an IV, but I sure would have liked one. There is possibly no better cure for a hangover than a few bags of IV fluid.

* * *

Once rehydrated, showered, and suited up, we hit the town once again, ready to celebrate our homecoming to the fullest extent of our capabilities. We decided to start out the evening by visiting a local Chinese restaurant. We left the hotel in two different vehicles, so most of the group

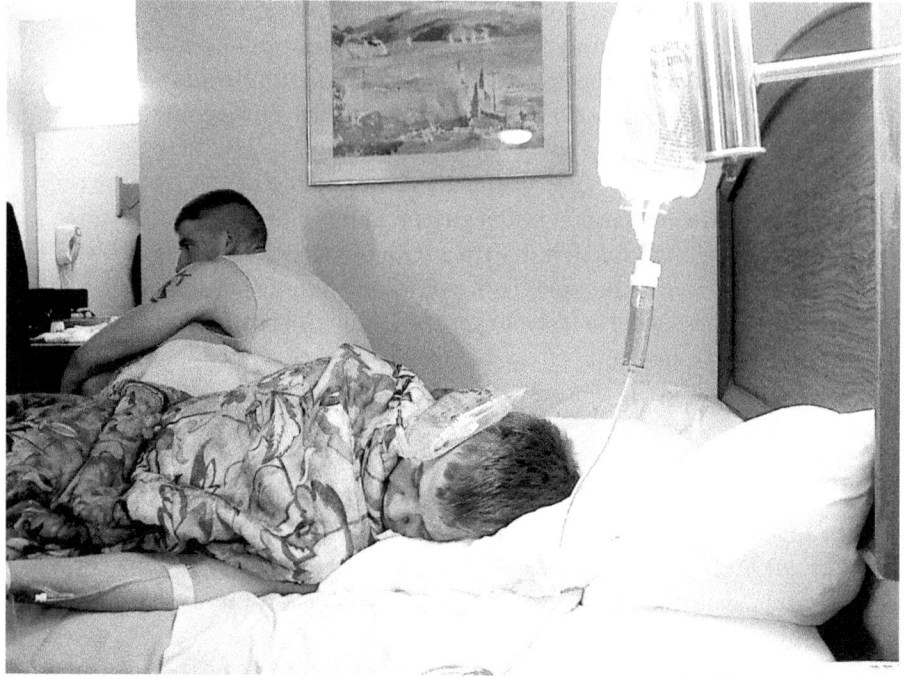

Lemmon resting while Chapman receives an IV after the 5K (courtesy Norman Blackman).

had arrived about twenty minutes before Blackman and me. They had texted me that they already had a table and to let the hostess know we were with the Thompson party. After Blackman parked the car, we both jumped out in our ridiculous suits and headed inside. Blackman walked through the restaurant door in front of me and headed to the center where the hostess stood behind a small podium. She was dressed in traditional Chinese attire and she stepped out to greet us with a bow as we approached.

Without slowing his stride, Blackman said, "Kim Joong kung pow some yung guy." Then he pointed to our group of friends in the corner. She just bowed and waved us past like she knew what he had said.

"Holy shit, you're an asshole," I said.

"What?" said Blackman.

"What? Do you speak Chinese?" I asked.

"No, but I'd like to," he replied.

"Holy shit, that was racist, dude," I said as we headed to the table.

"Well, what would you have said, Mister Culturally Sensitive?" Blackman asked as he pulled out his chair.

21. Superheroes with Drinking Problems

"I don't know. How about, Chinese if you prrease," I said with a chuckle.

We sat down to find everyone talking about where we should go for the night's festivities. Chapman was bound and determined to go to a strip club of some sort. Blackman and I agreed with him as we sat down. In reality everyone thought it was a great idea except for Thompson. Thompson hated strip clubs with a passion. He could often be found hiding in the bathroom when the dancers went around and tried to sell two-for-one dance specials. The rest of us, of course, thought this was hilarious and all the more reason to go. On top of that, we had promised Chapman we would show him the ropes in one of these fine establishments. Since we had promised Chapman, and because it would ruin Thompson's night, Blackman decided it was a done deal. We were going to Vixen's!

We finished our meal and headed for the door. Chapman was giddy with excitement in the cab ride over to the club.

"My problem is, I can never keep the ones out of my lap I don't want in it," said Chapman.

"You don't use the stripper block?" I asked.

"Stripper block?" Chapman said, perplexed.

"Yeah, you just throw your foot over your knee and hold your beer in your lap. The stripper block," said Thompson in a matter-of-fact tone.

"Then you just drop your defenses when a girl you want to talk to comes around, man," Blackman added.

Chapman smiled and nodded like we had just given him a million-dollar money-making secret.

* * *

After a short cab ride over, we jumped out of the cab, paid the doorman, and we were in it to win it. We all sat down in the corner of the club, ordered beers and shots, and prepared for the evening to get exciting. As we were sitting there, the girls started to move around the club looking for guys they could sell dances to. One such girl made her way straight toward Chapman. He was sitting in the front row with his defense down, just asking her to sit in his lap. They made eye contact as she was walking up, and I could tell by the look on his face, he wanted nothing to do with her.

"Hello, there," she said as she swung a feather boa over her shoulder, then turned to sit on his lap. Just as she got halfway down, Chapman threw his hand out, making a halt motion.

"Stop!" he said in a commanding voice.

She stopped halfway seated, then turned to look at him over her shoulder, both surprised and confused.

"Stripper Block, Engaged," he said as he threw his foot over his knee, placing his beer in his lap.

He looked around at us for approval, but all he got was laughter.

"You're not supposed to wait till they come up to do it, Chapman. Jesus!" said Thompson.

She, of course, stormed off, infuriated by Chapman's antics. It may not have been perfectly executed, but it accomplished the goal. Some days that's the best you can do.

As we sat in the strip club, we continued to drink excessively and to make total idiots of ourselves. We were buying a ridiculous number of lap dances for everyone, not just ourselves, and as a result, making a lot of friends both with the dancers and the customers. With each dance someone bought, the more ridiculous the dances became. Guys kept coming out of the VIP room with crazier and crazier stories of what the dancers were doing back there. I was certain that we would be thrown out of the place at any moment.

Chapman kept hearing these stories and stated, "Man, I have always wanted to fuck a stripper."

"Well, now's the best chance in your life," Blackman said with an excited fist pump.

With Blackman egging him on, Chapman got up, picked the nearest dancer and took her to the VIP room.

Blackman looked at me around the dancer in his lap and said, "Do you think he realizes that that stripper is seriously pregnant?"

"Probably not," Thompson replied.

As Chapman disappeared from our view, the song "Call Me Maybe" came on in the club and Blackman yelled, "This is my jam!"

He then leaped to his feet, vaulting the dancer who was sitting in his lap through the air. Before she landed, Blackman was already standing, doing some impromptu dance moves and fist pumps. The dancer landed on her ass, noticeably upset, but she acted like any professional stripper would: she stood up and strutted off to look for other drunks to entertain. After the song, we all sat back down, ordered more drinks, and blabbed on about everything and nothing.

Well after closing time, the club owner decided we needed to leave. He had kept the place open for well over two hours past closing time because we were spending so much money. On our way out, we ran into Chapman, who had his shirt unbuttoned and lipstick all over his face.

"Holy shit, did you fuck that pregnant stripper?" Blackman asked, way too loud.

"Better yet, did you know she was pregnant?" Thompson said, pointing at Chapman's stomach.

"Of course. I just killed two birds with one stone," Chapman said, smiling.

"What?" Blackman asked, confused.

"Oh yeah. My bucket list had 'fuck a stripper' and 'fuck a pregnant woman' on it. I say 'had,' because I just crossed them both off," Chapman stated, placing his hands on his hips proudly.

"Well, alrighty then," I said with a laugh.

Lemmon then put his arm around Chapman, guiding him out the door.

"Well, I am proud of you, ChipChap," Lemmon said in a fatherly tone.

We were stumbling out of the club to look for a cab when Lemmon spotted a gyro cart next to the road.

"We got to get some gyros, man! We got to!" said Lemmon.

"You're just going to get shit all over your suit, Lemmon. Wait till later and we will get some food back at our hotel." Thompson said.

"No, I won't fuck up my suit, man. Come on," said Lemmon.

"There is no stopping him," I thought, as we all followed him toward the cart. Once there, we all ordered some food and waited for our taxi to arrive.

As I was standing there eating my gyro, Thompson yelled, "Lemmon, man, what the hell are you doing!?"

Not wanting to miss out on what Lemmon was doing, I turned and looked behind me. He was aggressively trying to force his half-eaten gyro into the suit pocket on his vest. He just kept sliding it up and down over the pocket with serious intent.

"Dude! Those are not real pockets. They are just for looks," Thompson yelled.

Lemmon looked up at him with serious distrust, as if Thompson was trying to trick him in some way. He then slowly went back to eating the gyro, keeping an ever-watchful eye on Thompson.

"Holy shit! You are drunk," Chapman said, laughing as he flagged down the cab.

We then all climbed into the taxi and headed back to the hotel.

"I'm so hungry," said Lemmon on the ride back.

"Still?" I said. "You just ate a goddamn gyro."

"No, he didn't. He just rubbed it all over his thousand-dollar suit!" said Blackman.

"Hey, fuck you, man!" Lemmon yelled. "And we need some food, dammit, man!"

"There are no places open at this time, man. We were lucky to get gyros," I tried to explain.

"Well, we better figure it out. Use your sorcery to make a pizza like last time, hamp," said Lemmon, seriously concerned.

Once we got back to the hotel, Lemmon and Townsend decided that they would find some food somewhere if it killed them. So we left them in the lobby to their own devices. I was super-intoxicated and went straight to bed.

* * *

The next morning when I woke up, I was covered in crackers and chips, and there were refried beans smeared all over the nightstand on my side of the bed. As I got up, I looked around the room to discover that everyone was there apart from Blackman and Thompson. Still half asleep, I headed toward the bathroom to find Thompson in his boxers and suit jacket heating up cold pizza with a hairdryer.

Thompson looked at me, shrugged his shoulders and said, "There's no microwave, bro."

"What happened in here? It looks like a tornado hit a food truck," I said as I took in the damage.

"Close. Two drunk idiots bought out the food cart downstairs," Thompson replied, testing the texture of the pizza with his finger.

"What? They bought it out? The fucking bags of chips are like seven dollars apiece," I said, shocked.

"I know. They must have spent like $400 on snacks," Thompson said, taking his first bite.

"What a bunch of idiots," I thought as I headed to the bathroom. When I came back out into the main room, I realized the true extent of the damage. There were chips covering almost every surface of the room. Beans had been smeared all over the drapes and rubbed into the carpet. You could tell where Lemmon had fallen asleep on the floor because when he'd gotten up, he'd left a potato-chip outline of his body on the ground. Townsend was still asleep in the recliner in the corner with a burrito in each hand.

"How the fuck did I sleep through this?" I asked Thompson.

"Oh, you were crazy drunk," Thompson said as he finished off the pizza crust.

"So, what exactly happened in here, then?" I asked.

"Well, Townsend and Lemmon piled a bunch of bags of chips and burritos on the table right by your face and just went crazy," Thompson laughed. "Townsend was grabbing handfuls of chips and just smashing them into his mouth two hands at a time while Lemmon spilled burritos all over himself," said Thompson.

"Still wearing his suit?" I asked.

"Of course," Thompson replied, pointing to Lemmon, who was now sitting on the bed.

"And the drapes?" I asked.

"When I told Lemmon he was fucking up his suit again, he tried to wipe it and his hands off on the table, carpet, and finally the drapes," Thompson said, chuckling.

"Holy shit! Where is Blackman?" I asked.

"No clue," Thompson said, shrugging his shoulders.

After calling Blackman some thirty times with no response, we gave up and went downstairs to check out of the hotel and head to the nearest Waffle House. At the front desk, I realized just how much those snacks really cost. At first, I thought that there was something wrong with my bill. So, I showed it to the desk attendant and pointed to the $396.58 for amenities. Come to find out some of my friends had charged their refreshments to my room. The attendant tried to tell them that it was going to be quite expensive, but they assured him that they were "hard dick gunfighters" and that they could afford it. After angrily paying my bill, I rejoined the group by the door. Lemmon could tell I was pissed off, so he inquired as to my abrupt change in mood.

"Oh, nothing. The dude at the desk was just telling me that two 'hard dick gunfighters' charged $400 worth of burritos and chips to my fucking credit card, that's all," I said.

"Ohhh shit, Townsend!" Lemmon smirked, pointing at Townsend.

"You two pieces of shit are buying me breakfast ... for like a year," I said.

As Lemmon and I were bickering like old women, a different attendant came in the door that we were exiting and headed straight toward us.

"Will you guys please take your friend with you?" he asked with a pleading look.

"What friend?" asked Lemmon, noticeably confused.

"We are still missing Blackman," said Townsend.

"Oh yeah," Lemmon said, laughing.

"How do you know he is our friend?" asked Thompson.

"Well, he stumbled around outside for an hour yelling 'I fought in the war' and then climbed in the shrubs out front," said the attendant.

"Awesome!" I laughed.

"I was trying to wake him, but he demanded to be left alone stating that he was training for something called 'Ranger School.' I was just going to call the police now, but if you guys take him, I won't worry about it," he said.

"No problem, we got him, thanks," I said.

With that, we headed outside, collected Blackman, and went to the Waffle House.

– 22 –

Now Let's Never Do That Again

As I sat in the Waffle House drinking my eighth cup of coffee, I scanned this group of drunks in an attempt to take in the damage. Blackman was still in his suit from the night before and was covered in shrubbery, Lemmon had his suit pants on, dress shoes, and a flannel shirt, while the rest of us managed to dress like respectable drunks in the extra clothes we had brought. This is not to say that we looked any more respectable, since the headache that I had made me look like a man dying from a rapidly expanding brain tumor, and Chapman was lying on the bench seat waiting for his food to arrive. We all looked like we were at death's door just waiting for the reaper to take us. The funny thing is that we would go on to punish ourselves like this every weekend for the next several months. We had no problem spending thousands of dollars at a time, carelessly blowing all that hard-earned deployment money.

As the food arrived, Chapman rose up from the dead and Lemmon took his place, lying down on the bench seat. He only sat up once every few minutes to take a bite of his eggs and hash browns. I was still battling the worst headache of my life and couldn't yet muster the strength to eat anything. The table was full of eating noises and claims of being moments away from death.

"I ... am ... dying...," Townsend said slowly.

"I'll kill you halfway if you kill me all the way," Lemmon requested to anyone who would help.

"Hey! Blackman, where the fuck were you last night?" Chapman asked all of a sudden.

"I have three distinct memories from last night," Blackman began.

"Oh yeah, what are those?" Thompson asked.

"One being, Chapman knife-fighting a tree. The second was Lemmon ruining a perfectly good Italian suit," Blackman said.

"Hey, fuck you, man," Lemmon mumbled from the bench behind us.

"And the last thing that I remember was waking up in the grass out front of the Alpha Sigma sorority house," Blackman said, ignoring Lemmon and holding his head.

"That's it?" I asked.

"That's it, other than waking up in the shrubs out front of the hotel where I was apparently training for fucking Ranger School!" Blackman said, almost at a yell.

"Yeah, well, you're ready now, that's for sure," Lemmon laughed.

As we powered through breakfast, I started to realize just how futile our efforts in Afghanistan had been. Not only did we do nothing other than maintain superficial order in the region during our time there, but I later heard that the Taliban had taken our AO back less than a month after we turned it over to the replacing unit. As a matter of fact, our COIST guys had told me that they had lost control of two routes prior to our leaving KAF. This was not their fault, however, as they were only allotted a platoon to take over the workload of a company. Given the fact that we were stretched so thin, it would have been impossible for them to maintain the number of presence patrols that we did. I would be willing to wager that they could have stopped sleeping altogether and still not had enough hours in the day to do everything. They just did not have enough bodies to do it.

That understood, it is important to realize that the majority of people who live in Afghanistan do not have any idea why the United States is even there. They do not know about 9/11; they often do not even know who we are. I can remember going into a remote village to the east of our COP where the people there thought we were the Russians. They thought that the Russians had never left! As far as they are concerned, the United States is just another occupying force that they have to wait out. They are not looking to make changes; they are looking to survive, that's all. To them, this means waiting out whoever it is that is currently occupying their land, whether this be the United States, the Taliban, or the Russians.

The futility of this endeavor, however, does not in the slightest cheapen my reasons and experiences in country. I had, for as long as I can remember, wanted to know how I would act under such duress. I joined the Army to be a soldier, not to save the world. I was old enough and bitter enough when I joined the Army to realize that I would not be saving anything. With-

22. Now Let's Never Do That Again

out a doubt, I now know more about myself than I could have ever known if I had not joined. Not to mention that I made true friends in the Army, the kind of friends who you can call when you need help and will drive forty-three hours across country to help you. Not only will they do it, they will be happy to see you when they get there. I also learned to truly appreciate the gift that is being an American. It takes only a few short weeks of visiting a real third-world country to realize that you won the lottery if you were born in America. Most Americans take this gift for granted, and perhaps still so do I, but at least I realize how incredible this country is.

"Summerfield."

"Hey, Summerfield," Blackman said as he got my attention by hitting me on the shoulder.

"Hooooahh!" I said halfheartedly.

"Holy shit. I thought I was hung over," Lemmon laughed.

"What are you doing over there? You have just been staring at your eggs, bro," Blackman said and laughed.

"Oh, you know, just contemplating the futility of my very existence," I replied.

"Well, what you need to be doing is getting ready for some day drinking, you weak piece of shit! Because according to my phone, the B-team at the nearest strip club just punched in," Chapman said as he stabbed at his waffle.

"It's 0930!" Thompson said with noticeable disapproval.

"And?" Blackman asked, with just a hint of pretentiousness.

"They have bottomless mimosas," Chapman said, coaxing Thompson along.

"You had me at bottomless," Thompson said with a smile.

"There he is," said Blackman as he slapped me on the back.

"All right, well, I'm ready to go," I said as I stood up.

"Don't forget your tab, bro," Blackman said as he tried to hand me my ticket.

"Oh no, I don't pay for breakfast anymore. Give that shit to Lemmon," I said with a disgruntled look on my face.

Lemmon took the tab from Blackman, laughing to himself.

"How long do you think we can keep this up?" Thompson asked as he stood up from the table.

"Keep what up?" asked Chapman.

"Partying this hard," Thompson said as he approached the cashier.

"At this rate, I'll probably die before I run out of money, so it depends on your goal," I said, as I sat down by the door to avoid being crushed under the weight of my headache.

"I just need to drink till I forget the deployment or the Army in general, really," Blackman scoffed as he picked a piece of shrubbery out of his wallet.

"Yeah, let's never do that again," Lemmon said as he leaned up against the cash register.

"Let's not do what again?" Townsend asked as he came up behind Lemmon, who was now half lying on the register.

"Pretty much everything that we did in our lives before Friday," I said as serious as can be.

– 23 –

Bargaining for Your Future

April 11, 2015

    After what seemed like two days' worth of drunken war stories, Lemmon, Nate and I arrived at the dreaded Bargain Street. It was a short piece of asphalt barely 200 meters long. At the opposite end of the street stood one single lamppost flickering on and off. There was an extended stay motel on the right side of the road with a large vacancy sign proudly displayed out front. Directly across from the motel was a liquor store and small pawnshop, both of which were poorly lit and looked completely abandoned. Rounding the corner to the left, I was the first to step foot on the street of Bargains. As Lemmon followed behind me, we fell silent, scouring the shadows for ominous figures.
    "Why don't you guys like going down this road?" Nate asked as I continued to scrutinize the shadows.
    "Oh, you're about to find out," Lemmon said, halfheartedly motioning to three figures that had just materialized from the darkness.
    At a passing glance and under the cover of night, they appeared to be a group of scantily clad women, potentially prostitutes. But who am I to judge three half-naked women who just so happen to appear out of total darkness on the worst-lit road in town? Perhaps they were leaving the extended stay and headed out to paint the town red. Perhaps they were three upstanding citizens coming to see if we were lost and they just wanted to help.
    "Let me suck yo dick!" one of them yelled in a not-so-feminine voice.
    "Keep movin', they won't follow us into the light," I said as I quickened my pace.
    "I said let me get that dick," the leader of the group repeated.

As we shuffled along desperately trying to reach the single lamppost at the other end of the road, the three figures came into full view. Under the poorly lit storefront of the pawn shop, Nate could see exactly why Lemmon did not like this road. The three of them were all clearly men who had not made much of an attempt at transitioning to the fairer sex. At 5'11", 165 pounds, I am not an overly imposing figure. Lemmon and Nate, on the other hand, were both easily over 200 pounds. That said, all three of the ladies of the night were much more physically imposing than the three of us. The leader of the group looked like Terry Crews in a tube top and stilettos. The heels easily made him 6'5", and that miniskirt made it clear that Terry had not missed leg day in a really long time.

"Come on, don't be like that. Let me see that dick," the leader of the group repeated once again, more demanding than asking this time.

"I don't know if I should," Lemmon said in a shy playful voice while he held his hand over his mouth as if to cover a smile.

"Oh, you should," one of the girls said from the back of the group.

"Well, it is my birthday," Lemmon joked, making all six of us laugh.

"I do offer birthday deals," the group leader said as we reached the lamppost.

"I'll have to see how much money my grandma sent me this year and come back," Lemmon said as we rounded the corner to safety.

Relieved we had managed to escape the clutches of the evil Sherry Crews, we continued onward to our final destination. Lemmon's ridiculous interaction with the group kept us laughing for quite some time. With the dreaded Bargain Street behind us, Vixen's was now just a short mile walk away. All we had to do was fight off a few regular prostitutes, tell a few drug dealers no thank you, and we would be at the finest gentlemen's club in the state of North Carolina. Once we made visual contact with the club, Lemmon realized that all three of us had knives in our pockets. Knowing that they had just started searching people at the door, we had to come up with a plan.

"Not only that, but they are not going to let me in," Nate said, looking at his pants and shirt.

"Why?" Lemmon asked in a stern tone.

"Why? My right pant leg is torn all the way up to my knee, there are holes in my shirt, and all three of us are drenched in sweat. Not to mention Eddie's got grass stains all over his back from 38 unnecessary ninja rolls," Nate said, sticking his chin out and looking at me unimpressed.

"Aww, you greatly overestimate the dress code at this fine establishment," Lemmon said as he motioned toward the club.

23. Bargaining for Your Future

While they were arguing, I had a brilliant idea. All I had to do was take my knife out of my pocket and then use the clip on the handle to stow it behind my pants button. I was certain that they would not pat me down right over my crotch. I then proudly showed my concealment tactics to Lemmon and Nate. Lemmon thought I was a damn genius, while Nate proved to be more difficult to impress. Despite Nate's skepticism, the three of us hid our knives and we made our way to the door. I went first so as to show the other two just how ingenious my idea had been. The bouncer patted all my pockets and the sides of my belt line, then let me right on in. I promptly handed the cashier a ten-dollar bill and turned back towards Nate. I then gave him a confusingly obvious nod with a huge smile on my face. The bouncer just thought I was a drunk idiot (which I was) and let the three of us on in.

Stepping out of the entryway, we beheld Vixen's in all her splendor. The club was constructed in an S shape with the main bar on the right side of the first bend and the main stage in the middle of the second. After I allowed her ambiance to take me in its warm embrace, the three of us each ordered a beer. Once our drinks arrived, we started contemplating the idea of more shots.

"I'll drink anything but Jack," Lemmon said as he watched me size up the bottles behind the counter.

"You don't like Jack?" Nate said with a funny look on his face.

"I don't have a problem with Jack. I just don't like Vixen's version of it. It's like they go around the club at the end of the night and empty all of the unfinished drinks into a bucket. Then they wring out the bar rags into it for some extra zest. At which time they erroneously call it Jack," Lemmon explained as he grabbed a dirty bar rag off the counter and shook it at Nate.

While Lemmon was explaining to Nate how the sausage gets made, I got the bartender's attention and ordered us three double shots of the best damn Jack Daniels money can buy. I set one in front of each of the three of us. Knowing full well that Lemmon would not turn down an alcoholic beverage on principle, I waited to see his reaction.

"Is this Jack? Goddammit, man. Well, when you're puking the night away, it's your own fault," Lemmon said as he threw the shot down his throat and gritted his teeth.

"Oh, I'll be fine," I said as I downed my shot and desperately tried to maintain a straight face.

As I stood there and stared at Lemmon, I did my best to contort my face into something that vaguely appeared to be a comfortable expression.

On the inside, however, the double shot of Jack was devastating my digestive system. I was going to vomit. It wasn't a matter of if, but only a matter of where. So I calmly asked Lemmon to order me another shot and told him that I needed to relieve myself. I bid them farewell with a tip of an imaginary hat and calmly walked away.

I could not have arrived in the bathroom a moment later. Within steps of the first urinal, I released an explosion of projectile vomit that violently spewed against a worn-out porcelain toilet. I have never vomited so much and for so long in my life. Not even when I was in Kotizi dry-heaving cranberries was it this bad. I vomited for so long into the urinal I feared that it was going to overflow and spill out onto my shoes. In an attempt at keeping my problem off the floor, I decided to utilize the unoccupied urinal to my right. As I redirected fire into the second urinal, I spewed a constant stream of projectile vomit. The disgusting green beam ricocheted and splattered continuously out of the first urinal across three feet of tile and finally into the empty urinal next to me. It looked like some kind of weird anime character's special attack.

After a solid three more streams, I finally started to regain some composure. I then desperately searched for whatever remnants of dignity I had stored away for a rainy day. Somewhat composed, I awkwardly made my way to the sink, where I started to clean myself up. All I had to do was make myself appear presentable to a bunch of drunks in a dark room. Hunching over the sink, I felt something digging into my pelvis. Searching the area, I found the knife that I had so cleverly hidden behind the button on my pants. Just as I was clipping it back in my left pocket where it belonged, another patron entered the bathroom. He was absolutely mortified to see the mess that I had created.

"What in the hell is going on in here! This is disgusting!" the man yelled as he took in the devastation.

"I know. Some people, right?" I said as I wiped my mouth, trying to appear as if I had not just vomited a five-gallon bucket of green sludge onto the bathroom floor.

"How does someone clog two toilets with puke!? Why not use the stall? I don't understand what I'm looking at," he said as he attempted to sneak past the mess on the floor to where the stalls were located.

"I'll let someone know there is a mess in here," I said as I exited the bathroom to rejoin Lemmon and Nate at the bar.

Back at the bar, a massive Jager bomb awaited me. At this point the mere sight of booze was unsettling, but I was determined to maintain my ruse of invincibility. So, I strutted up, grabbed the plastic cup and forced

23. Bargaining for Your Future

it down. The very instant that Jager bomb hit my stomach, it detonated! Desperately searching for a reason to turn away from Lemmon, I grabbed my beer and headed to the seating area. As I rounded the main stage, I did some impromptu Lamaze breathing techniques in an attempt to contain the JDAM that just went off in my sensitive little tummy. As I struggled to calm my stomach, I scouted the area for some open spots. I found three upholstered chairs and plopped down in the middle one. I wanted to be able to talk to both Nate and Lemmon without having to yell over the music. This was a tactical decision more than a social one, as I feared overexerting my diaphragm yelling could be disastrous. I needed to do everything within my power to keep from unleashing my devastating anime attack on the dancer in front of us.

After we all sat down and got comfortable, I threw my right leg over my left. This was, of course, done to engage the ever popular and highly effective stripper block. Nate followed suit, since he was in no mood for company. Doing so revealed the totality of damage his pants had suffered. As he set his right ankle on his left knee, it was as if his pants stayed in place perpendicular to the floor. At a quick glance it looked like he had either both feet on the ground or his stripper block engaged. One had to look closely to figure out just what kind of optical illusion he was working with.

"Fuck ... you," Nate said while I snickered and pretended to look away from his dangling pant leg.

While my attention was on Nate's fashion statement, Chardonnay convinced Lemmon that he needed a private dance. Taking him by the hand, she led him back to the VIP section of the club. As he exited the main area, I came to a hilarious realization. Every one of us had a knife in his pants. Yet I had decided that the best way to deal with Nate's pants being stuck on that fence was to violently and repeatedly stomp on his leg. I had considered sharing this gem with Nate, but decided he was grumpy enough without that floating around out there. So I just sat quietly and pretended to drink my beer.

After quite some time, Lemmon finally came limping back to where we were seated.

"That must have been some dance, Lemmon. You were back there for like an hour," I said as I wondered what feminine wiles that woman had used to seduce poor old Lemmon.

"It was the worst dance I have ever had in my entire life!" Lemmon scoffed as he shook one of his legs out with a painful grimace on his face.

"Well, why did you stay back there so long, then?" I asked with a confused hand gesture.

"I had to prove to her just how fuckin' tough I was," Lemmon answered in a mocking tone.

"Tough?" I questioned him, even more confused than before.

"Oh yeah, I'm tough," Lemmon said as he motioned for us to follow him to the parking lot.

✳ ✳ ✳

Once the three of us were in a cab out front, Lemmon began to regale us of his battle with the fierce and powerful Chardonnay. Apparently when she started dancing and grinding on his lap, she noticed that he was grimacing. Not wanting to cause him any more pain, she stopped to ask him if she was hurting him. Being the tough paratrooper he was, he told her she couldn't hurt him. Just to punctuate his sentiment, he pointed out that she didn't weigh a hundred pounds soaking wet. This, of course, prompted her to attack him with an even more aggressive barrage of bounces and grinding maneuvers. Despite his attempts at hiding it, the attacks were obviously taking their toll on our hero. At the end of each song, she kept asking him if he wanted to stop or buy another dance.

"To prove to her how tough I was, I just kept buying dances and acting like it was the most fun I had had in my entire life," Lemmon told us.

After Lemmon could no longer take it, he jumped up and explained to her that he would buy another dance, but he didn't have the money. He then assured her that next time he comes in he would show her what was up.

"So why were the dances so painful?" I asked Lemmon, still unsure as to what had happened.

"Well, like a complete idiot, I forgot to move this goddamn knife back to my pocket. Sooo, she was grinding steel and kydex into my groin over and over again," Lemmon said as he snatched the knife from his pocket and waved it in my face.

As the story came to an end, we arrived at my apartment, where we started getting ready for bed. After throwing a few blankets on the couch for the two of them, I headed into the kitchen. Once there I found my bottle of melatonin gummies and ate a few of them. Being the inquisitive troop that he was, Lemmon picked the bottle up and examined it. He couldn't believe that they made fruit snacks that would help you sleep! So he decided that he was going to have a handful or two, since he hadn't had a good night's sleep since before the war.

Knowing full well he shouldn't have eaten more than three, I put the bottle back on the shelf above the sink. My only goal was to try to get some

23. Bargaining for Your Future

sleep. Nate and I needed to be up in four hours so I could ship him off to Basic Training. No sense wasting any time scolding Lemmon over gummy bears.

* * *

The sound of my alarm going off at 0600 was one of the most offensive things I have ever heard. It quite literally abraded my eardrums. Dragging myself out of bed, I found Nate awake at the kitchen table drinking coffee. Lemmon, on the other hand, was strung out on the floor in a position a contortionist would not envy. In his hand was that bottle of melatonin gummies. Apparently, he had gotten up and eaten some more of them for some reason. Grabbing the bottle away from him, I could see a pile of half-eaten gummies in his other hand.

"Did he eat more of those things?" I asked Nate as I nudged Lemmon's motionless body.

"I told him not to, but he's Lemmon," Nate laughed to himself while sipping his coffee.

Me sitting in a fighting position for the last time in my military career (courtesy Brandon Young).

I wasted a good twenty minutes trying to wake Lemmon up, since he had made me promise to take him with us. He wanted to personally ship Nate off to Basic Training. It was a futile endeavor, as the combination of booze and melatonin had rendered him catatonic. I was barely able to elicit a few speech-like sounds out of him before it was time to go.

The car ride to the recruiting office was silent other than a few sighs of exhaustion. Once there, I parked the car in a spot near the already waiting bus that would lead Nate to years of regret and despair. After a few brief moments, we both stepped out of the car, and Nate prepared to face his destiny.

"Let's not make this one of those heartfelt goodbyes. It doesn't suit you," Nate said, looking at me and smiling.

"I will wear that holey shirt you made on that fence to your graduation," I told Nate as I shook his hand.

Nate just smiled, nodded and boarded the bus.

He left for Basic Training the day I got out of the Army. Just when our poor mother thought she was done worrying, Nate had to go and fuck it all up. Just the thought of this made me laugh out loud.

Getting back into my decrepit old Ford, I started it up, put it in gear and drove away from the recruiting office. I was now a free man. No more eight-hour-long formations. No more 0530 wakeups. No more fighting positions. Just the sweet, sweet taste of freedom.

Index

Alonzo 109, 141, 153
ALP 31, 33, 38, 116, 117, 130
ANA 29, 30, 42, 45, 46, 59, 63, 76, 140
Amardad 71, 93, 101, 135

Bargain Street 11, 185
Barns 123
Bertelli 22, 49, 64, 103, 104, 120
Big Al's Tavern 10
Blackman 58, 105, 117, 151, 155, 162, 169, 174, 176, 179, 181, 182
Blast in Place (BIP) 32, 43, 141, 151
bounding overwatch 100

Callen 123
camel spider 95
Chapman 115, 130, 165, 166, 172, 175, 176, 177
Cole, Deegan (DC) 80, 110, 134, 137, 138, 159
conventional fire and maneuver 24
Cristo 61, 63, 67, 81, 123

Denton 36, 93, 99, 110
Doc Gio 40, 66, 73, 77, 78, 101, 107, 111, 124, 144, 147, 173
Douglas 35, 64, 77, 85, 90, 144
Doxycycline 91

ECP 51
18X-ray 19
enemy TTPs 24

5k 170
Fourth Floor Club 166

grape rows 78
Gundi Ghar 89, 119

Harris 54, 102, 110
Henderson 130
Hudson 90
Hunter 20, 24, 25, 29, 44, 52, 55, 57, 58, 59, 62, 75, 76, 88, 89, 103, 115, 117, 126

IED 33, 36, 76, 120, 124, 141, 149
IED belt 30

Kandahar Airfield 26, 155
King 42, 120, 150, 151

Lee 160
Lemmon 9, 22, 43, 60, 93, 98, 113, 122, 123, 146, 167, 170, 172, 177, 186, 190
LMTV 133

Magnum 160
MATV 27
MaxxPro 54
McCance 36
MedEvac 74, 101, 125, 129, 146
Mine Hound Training 25
Mine Roller 27
Murphy 91, 109

Nadey 90
Nalgham 27
Nate 9, 12, 16, 17, 185. 189, 191, 192
Nolan 90, 108
NTC 22, 23

Odinson 98, 99, 104, 116, 142

Index

Packing List: Dick Moutain 30; Kotizi 56; Gundi Ghar 88
Palmer 105
Park 100
PL 38, 40, 101, 113, 121, 122, 126, 136
PSG 31, 38, 113, 114

Rodriguez 97, 102, 112, 173

Sanders 49, 53, 54, 70, 73, 74, 82, 83, 104, 111, 123
SEEK 82
Suicide Bomber 122
Sullivan 21, 30
Swoyer 53, 78, 99, 111, 112, 113

Tabish 140
Thompson 95, 100, 162, 163, 167, 175, 177, 178, 183
THOR 96
Tillers 152, 154
Townsend 33, 37, 52, 54, 55, 84, 85, 99, 107, 108, 110, 112, 131, 170, 173
2–321 97

Vixen's 11, 175, 187

Walker 149, 152, 154
Wilson 120, 140, 143, 144, 145, 146

Young 46, 62, 109